Advance Praise for *And* Then *I'll Be Happy!*:

"Any woman who wants to find out how she may be sabotaging her happiness needs this book!"

—Carolyn Chambers Clark, Ed.D., author of
Living Well with Anxiety and *Living Well with Menopause*

"Remember *Goldilocks and the Three Bears*? Nothing was ever good enough for that girl! A master observer of women and relationships, Kristen Houghton uses her funny, warm, and deeply engaging style to open us up to the ways that we, as women, chronically postpone and deny our own happiness. As a clinical psychologist, I constantly see women in states of depression, low self-esteem, and body hatred. I am grateful to Kristen, who masterfully gets past our defensiveness to show us new ways to discover self-acceptance, inner peace and happiness. Thank you, Kristen, for your groundbreaking book. It's about time someone addressed the concerns felt deeply in our hearts and showed us innovative, insightful ways to heal them! This book is a must read for any woman who puts herself last on her exhaustive 'to do' list."

—Maria Rago, Ph.D., Clinical Director, Rago & Associates Counseling
Center; psychological consultant for women's issues

"Kristen Houghton is truly an inspiring writer, one whose 'girlfriend therapy' is the best kind of advice any woman can receive. She is candid, up-to-the minute on what today's woman needs, and spices up her prose with a humor we can all use in our lives. Her writing is unparalleled in this arena, and her advice motivates her readers. All women need to read this book, and read it now! It is fresh, and filled with solid advice for anyone who has, as Kristen Houghton so perfectly writes, found happiness to be elusive in their lives."

—Diane Lang, M.S.W., adjunct professor of psychology, Montclair State
University; therapist, Livingston Institute of Psychology;
author of *Baby Steps: The Path from Motherhood to Career*

"Kristen Houghton's writing thrives as she creates compelling articles for her nationally syndicated *Relationship* column. Her insight into relationship problems and their solutions is brilliant! Humorous, realistic, and st relationship writer out there."

—Greg Archer, *San Francisco Examiner*

"Kristen's heartfelt perspectives are seasoned with frankness and wisdom, yet are boldly refreshing. Her advice, when heeded, will help you revive a relationship, reinvent your life, and make positive changes! This book on women and happiness is one I recommend wholeheartedly. It is an insightful, wonderful dose of reality. Great writing!"
—Bill Mitchell, the 7 Day Detective, author of
The More You Know: Getting the Evidence and Support
You Need to Investigate a Troubled Relationship

"With a sharp, witty persona, Kristen Houghton tackles relationship building with humor. Her material is at times eye-popping, getting her message and guidance across with a juicy tone that garners attention. I suspect we'll be hearing a lot from her in 2009 as we all battle the recession, try to keep a handle on our relationships, and attempt to keep a smile on our faces."
—Judy Martin, Emmy Award–winning broadcast journalist, reporter
for National Public Radio; writer/radio anchor at CNBC Radio

"Kristen Houghton is a brilliant writer who always writes timely and informative features. I look forward to reading her column on a daily basis—I never know what the articles are going to be about, but I know I can always expect a clever and entertaining story written by an expert in the field. Writing a book that encourages women to attain their goals and find their own happiness was the next logical step for Kristen. Her book is a definite must read!"
—Danielle Duff, columnist, *Washington Examiner*

And *then* I'll Be Happy!

Stop Sabotaging Your Happiness and Put Your Own Life First

KRISTEN HOUGHTON

Foreword by Janet Taylor, MD

life

Guilford, Connecticut

An imprint of Globe Pequot Press

GPP Life is an imprint of Globe Pequot Press.

Designed by Sheryl P. Kober

Library of Congress Cataloging-in-Publication Data
Houghton, Kristen.
  And then I'll be happy! : stop sabotaging your happiness and put your own life first / Kristen Houghton.
     p. cm.
  ISBN 978-0-7627-5433-5
  1. Women—Psychology. 2. Happiness. I. Title. II. Title: And then I'll be happy!
  HQ1206.H68 2010
  155.3'33—dc22

                                                    2009029480

Printed in the United States of America

10 9 8 7 6 5 4 3 2 1

Contents

Acknowledgments

While the author is the one putting words to paper, no book ever truly gets written without some help from others. In my case there are many people to whom I owe a debt of gratitude.

First and foremost, many, many thanks go to my wonderful literary agent, Stacey Glick, vice president of Dystel and Goderich Literary Agency. Her patience, her expertise, her encouragement, and her calmness kept this writer on track. She always took time out of her incredibly busy schedule to answer any questions I may have had. From the bottom of my heart, I thank you, Stacey.

To Mary Norris, my editor at Globe Pequot, who was amazingly helpful, unfailingly patient, and brilliant in all her advice and kindness to a fledgling author; many, many thanks.

To Ellen Urban, project editor, and Laura Jorstad, editor, for doing such a wonderful job with the final version of my book.

To the wonderful women who came forward to tell me the stories about their search for happiness, this book was written for you and could not have come about without you.

To Michele Ferris, Eldo Varghese, and Davon Cannon— true friends who believed in me right from the beginning and whose support I treasure.

And finally, to the green-eyed teenage boy I met one May night, who became the man who became my husband. Alan, I am so grateful for all your patience, love, and support while writing this book. I love you!

Believe in yourself and never, *never* be afraid to try.

—KH

Foreword

And Then *I'll Be Happy!* is a book that all women need to read. Many of us spend too much time and precious energy focused on the complicated and frequently unfulfilling challenge of looking out for others while believing that the key to our happiness is not within our own grasp. This external focus misdirects our physical resources and can deplete our emotional reserves away from the real source of our happiness—ourselves. We have all done what the women in this book have done: put our own personal happiness and satisfaction on hold in order to take care of other people's problems or situations. There is a definite need for women to maintain a healthy balance among work, family, and self—we can and should empower ourselves to live complete and fulfilling lives. In my practice I frequently work with women who struggle with the same issue. They are not able to say no to family, friends, or coworkers and yes to their own needs. The end result is a constant feeling of bitterness, a veil of resentment, and a lack of joy and fulfillment.

By understanding how only we have the ability to build our own happiness, we can allow ourselves to be happy. Kristen Houghton is disarmingly honest and realistic in her writing and spot-on advice. She laces her advice with enough humor to alleviate the stress of real-life situations, but never strays far from the good solid solutions she offers in this book.

In my work as a psychiatrist in private practice in New York City and as a frequent contributor on CNN and the *Today* show on NBC, I have met women who are very much like the ones in this book. No matter what their age, socioeconomic status, or ethnicity, women have a tendency to place themselves last in their own lives. *And* Then *I'll Be Happy!* offers a guide for women to reflect on difficult life lessons while realizing how to reclaim our authentic happy selves. I thoroughly enjoyed reading it and I highly recommend it to my friends and my patients.

—Janet Taylor, M.D., psychiatrist and clinical instructor in psychiatry at Columbia University. Dr. Taylor is also a contributor to *O, The Oprah Magazine* and *Family Circle* magazine.

Introduction:
The Elusive State of Happiness

You've done it again. You sacrificed your own happiness trying to make someone else happy. You assigned your happiness, one more time, to some future date, "in a galaxy far, far away."

Hey, it's no big deal, your happiness can wait. After all, you have to make sure everyone else in your life is happy before you even can consider being so! Only good little girls who sacrifice their lives for every single person in their small universe are allowed to be happy, right?

It is also possible that you may be a "settler"—a woman who feels she may never get what she wants and so sabotages her chances for happiness by settling for less than she should have. It is unfortunately too common a practice for women. You may settle for less of a relationship, less of a career, less of a home, all because you feel that what you really want is way out of your range. In settling you undermine your prospects for happiness and become another woman who thinks that she will be happy sometime, somehow in the future. Some women settle for marriage and motherhood because they're told that this is what they *should* want. But not all women are cut out to be wives and mothers. Settling for what others tell you that you should have shortchanges your own life's value.

Perhaps you're trying to be the "perfect" woman who has it all, does it all well, and never makes a mistake in anything. After all, you're a woman, and you are told that in the twenty-first century you not only can but absolutely must have it all! Perfect wife, perfect mother, perfect job; everything perfect including your mental breakdown from trying to keep up with all that perfection!

Maybe you have a victim mentality, blaming fate and others for your unhappiness. You see yourself as a someone who shouldn't even try, and yet you hope that by some crazy miracle, happiness is waiting for you "somewhere out there"—future tense, of course.

Have you been conditioned to see happiness only as a future reward? It starts in childhood. Your parents tell you:

"Be a good girl while we're shopping and we'll stop for ice cream."

"I'll give you a dollar for every A you get on your report card."

"If you're nice to your cousin while she's visiting, I'll buy you whatever you want."

The message is clear: Only after you do something good will you deserve to get something you want. It continues all through your school years and into your professional life. People tell you that if you do something now, you'll be rewarded later. Work hard, harder, hardest; be good, better, best. Sacrifice the present for the future! It is hardly surprising that you feel you shouldn't be happy if you haven't been "good"!

Or perhaps you bought into the fairy tales fed to you by society and the media that tell you exactly when you can be happy. You know the messages: When you're the right size, when you drive the right car, when you use the right deodorant, blah-blah-blah, the list goes on and on. Your happiness date is determined by what some highly paid marketing team, well schooled in the techniques of brainwashing, tells you it should be. "You'll be happy when we say you can be happy and not a minute before, damn it!"

But you're intelligent; you like to think of yourself as a smart, modern woman with a good mind of your own. You fix problems, you run businesses, you make decisions; you're independent. So *tell* me, intelligent, smart, modern woman with a mind of your own—why do you keep sabotaging your life and your happiness? What sinister marker in your DNA makes you a glutton for the punishment of sacrificing yourself for others or for believing you must postpone happiness until the exact "right time"? You are the "unworthy one," a woman who never feels she deserves to be happy until she has met the criteria for success. Unfortunately those criteria are usually conceived and written by someone else who really knows nothing at all about you. You are being duped.

The biggest problem is that, whether you are the good girl or the unworthy one, you keep sabotaging your chances for happiness all by yourself with no help from anyone else. And then you wonder why you're never happy!

Since there is no equivalent of a Google search for the state of happiness, we have to find our own way. Let's look for that maddeningly elusive state of happiness together. It is closer and easier to find than you think.

The idea for this book came about as most life-altering changes usually do. It began as a nagging feeling in the back of my mind that I was never truly happy; that I was waiting to be happy. One of the reasons was that, in order for me to actually be happy, I assumed everything had to be perfect in my life—everything from relationships to career to personal appearance.

And because everything was never "perfect," I put off any thoughts of real happiness until some vague future date. Things I wanted to do, I placed in the future, telling myself I would do this or that when the time was right, and, of course, the time never was right. At least I didn't think so.

All my life happiness was a state that was destined to happen for me "sometime in the future." Most of my future happiness was predicated on the when-this-happens-then-I'll-be-happy type of thinking. You know the phrases we all use:

"When I'm free to do what I want to do, then I'll be happy."

"When I'm doing the work I love, then I'll be happy."

"When I have more money, then I'll be happy."

"When I stop being afraid to try, then I'll be happy."

"When my lousy luck changes, then I'll be happy."

"When I'm in a loving relationship, then I'll be happy."

"When I'm living where I want to live, then I'll be happy."

"When there's no stress in my life, then I'll be happy."

"When my family is happy, when my children are successful, then I'll be happy."

"When my boyfriend/fiancé/husband changes, then I'll be happy."

And of course the ever-popular universal women's condition for happiness:

"When I finally lose this damn weight, oh boy, then I'll *really* be happy!"

The list for me personally went on and on and, unfortunately, so did the years. My happiness was elusive. I felt frustrated that I couldn't be happy because none of my conditions for happiness were being met. I blamed my lack of happiness on not being who and not having what I wanted. The idea of happiness for me was comparable to the old farmer's trick of holding a carrot to the nose of a horse to get the animal to follow him anywhere he went. The carrot in my case represented happiness.

Faithfully I followed that "carrot," but unlike the horse, I never got to enjoy it.

Hoping for a perfect future, I was creating a present where happiness was nonexistent. I never felt happy. It was really ironic that I wasn't a happy person because, as the syndicated relationships columnist for a prestigious national news magazine, I gave advice in my articles on how to create and have happy relationships.

I could write and speak about how couples could achieve happiness in their lives, yet the very happiness I spoke, and wrote, about always seemed to elude me in my own life and relationships.

Finally I decided to write an article for my column questioning why happiness was always so hard to attain.

The Elusive State of Happiness

Are *you* happy? Neither am I.

What exactly is happiness and how do we achieve it? Is it a gift we give to ourselves or is it part of a reward system? The intangible state of simply being happy is hard to find, and there are no maps or GPS trackers to help us chart a course.

My husband tells me I don't *allow* myself to be happy. The word allow grates on my nerves and annoys me no end. Who doesn't allow themselves to be happy?! I ask him.

"*You* don't," he says. "Being simply happy is difficult for you and it shouldn't be. Everyone deserves to be happy, but you don't allow it."

Stated like that, I grudgingly concede that there might be a modicum, just a very small kernel, of truth in what he says.

Happiness has always been an elusive state for me. It is always "somewhere out there" in my future. There is some truth to the statement that I don't allow myself happiness. It isn't that I don't enjoy my life to an extent; it's just that I always feel happiness is a reward for being "good." For meeting that deadline, for losing those ten pounds, for being the good girl who does everything right. I can't really begin to be happy until my life has met certain conditions, and those conditions vary according to where I am. Home, work, leisure; every area has its own unique criteria for how and when I can be happy.

I truly believe women have a harder time permitting themselves to be happy than men do. We're people pleasers and, while that is great for our families, our co-workers, our friends, it is not at all good for us. Unlike men, we put our happiness last on the list. This is not to imply that our males are not giving creatures; they are. But happiness seems to come easier for them than for us. Their happiness is definitely not last on their to-do list.

Men take pleasure in small, everyday things. For some reason women don't, won't, or can't. We are too busy being "the good little girl" who must make sure everyone around us is happy first. Or worse, we see ourselves as an "unworthy," not deserving of happiness until certain goals, usually totally unattainable and defined by others, are met.

Women fall victim to what I call the Goldilocks Syndrome: Everything in our lives must be "just right" in order for us to be happy. Of course everything is never "just right." Life isn't like that. Ask any woman who has ever been the center of attention in a public setting; a work presentation or ceremony, for example. Even if everyone assures her she was fantastic, she will be the one who notices the minute mistake she made or something she forgot to do or say. Nothing is ever "just right."

How we view happiness is a prime factor in achieving it. Are we looking for ecstatic, jumping-for-joy happy? Are we saying that once a certain thing happens, we won't ever be unhappy again? That is fairy-tale thinking.

Despite whatever is going on in our lives, happiness isn't something we should be putting on hold until certain things are right. Happiness should be attainable. It should be a feeling of satisfaction and joy for the good parts of your life and the knowledge that you are not just hanging around, waiting for something fantastic *to happen*.

But that is exactly what I do.

Making "being happy" conditional will never work. Trying to reach some unrealistic goal set by someone else won't fly, either. Conditions and other people cannot define or create happiness for us, only we can. It should be as natural a state as breathing. It should be, absolutely, but that is not how it is.

What do I want? As women, what do we want? We're twenty-first-century independent women! What will make us embrace happiness as easily as we embrace other aspects of our lives? Why can't we be happy, damn it?! By all accounts, I should be happy. I am lucky enough to do work that I truly love and to be successful at it. I'm married to a funny, wonderful man, have good friends and a great lifestyle. So what is it that stops me from being happy? I have no idea.

If happiness is an intangible state of being, then for me it may very well be ever elusive and hidden from sight. And I don't want that to be. I want to be happy.

Quite frankly, I'm unhappy that I'm not happy. How about you?

That article took on a life of its own. I received an unbelievable number of emails and letters about the "happiness problem."

From women in professional organizations to stay-at-home moms and including women from all traditions and backgrounds, everyone seems to see their own happiness as a future occurrence and not something available, or even *possible,* in the here and now. There seem to be as many reasons for a woman to not be happy as there are people in the world.

And then there are the men, who tell me they are worried about their wives, girlfriends, fiancées, daughters, mothers; wondering why happiness is so lacking for the women in their lives.

Feeling "simply happy" is something women find almost impossible to do. But the question is, why?

Women have certainly made great strides in the workforce and in many high-earning professions. Many of us perform an incredible balancing act with families and work. We are accomplished people who should have a great deal of satisfaction and happiness. Why, then, the thinking that "I cannot be happy until . . . "?

And what if "until . . ." never happens?

The conditions for happiness are many, and they are as varied as the women seeking it. Some see happiness coming through the men and children in their lives, other people who will somehow make them happy. They see sacrificing their own lives for others *now* as a means of ensuring happiness *later on.*

Others think that a certain lifestyle will bring happiness, while still others see it as achieving the "right" kind of success in their work, a yardstick for success created by someone else. Then there are those, like me, who feel undeserving of it. We see the state of happiness only as a reward for a personal goal—one that may not ever be met because it is unrealistic.

Happiness is our right.
And yet we feel it is perfectly all right to put our own happiness on hold until certain things are perfect. Making happiness conditional will never work. Conditions and other people cannot define or create happiness for us; only we can. We have to learn to be happy. It sounds so ridicu-

lous to say we have to *learn* how to be happy; it should be a natural state. It *should* be, but for far too many women that is not the case.

Can and should we be happy without everything being just right?

The answer to this is an unequivocal yes! Reality check: There will never be a time when every single thing in your life is completely perfect. If you wait for that to occur, you'll be doing nothing *but* waiting.

Is there a secret to happiness?

Yes and no; it depends on your definition of the word secret. Happiness is not generic. No one can identify completely what your personal idea of happiness should be. You are the CEO of the business known as you; only you have the secret to your own brand of happiness. What do you want for yourself?

That is the true secret.

How do we even begin to achieve this simple nine-letter word, which the dictionary defines as "the quality or state of being happy, a contentment, a joy"?

Read that definition carefully. How attainable is that quality or state for you? In fact it's much easier than you think; like a contented baby who wakes up smiling every morning, the state of happiness is more attainable than you know.

In this book we will search for, and find, that state of being. You will read the real-life* stories of women who

---

*The women's names have been changed. All interviews were conducted with the author's express guarantee that each woman's privacy would be respected. This has been done.

all said . . . And Then I'll Be Happy. They set conditions and rules for happiness. Each woman had her own idea of what it would take for her to be happy, and each one, including me, didn't find the happiness she thought was waiting. Changes had to be made.

There's a key for everything.
For each tale of happiness never achieved there is a solution, a simple key for what each woman could have done. If you recognize yourself in these tales, please know that you don't have to wait for happiness; you already have the potential for it. Just look around you. The key to happiness is in your possession. All you have to do is learn how to use it to unlock negative mind-sets.

Is there one personal key to unlocking the chains of negativity that keep us prisoners in our own minds? My grandfather obviously thought so. He was a master locksmith and a philosopher of sorts who not only made locks and keys but related them to everyday life.

I once watched him working intently to open a particularly stubborn lock on an old chest of drawers. He used one key after another; some he discarded immediately. Finally he found one that he thought could be fitted to the lock and began to grind it to the lock's specifications. He kept at it until he had the perfect fit of key and lock. The owner of the chest of drawers was amazed and delighted at what my grandfather had been able to do. So was I. It seemed almost magical.

But my grandfather later told me there was no magic to it at all. "Honey, there is no lock that can't be opened.

You just have to find, or make, the right key for it. But first you need to get rid of the keys that *don't* work."

This is also true for unlocking your potential for happiness: You have to find the correct key to use. As with metal locks, everyone uses a different type of key made expressly for their own lives, grinding it until it can perfectly turn the lock.

Keys are only magical and work if you use them. A locked drawer doesn't open itself even if the right key is lying next to it. Ideas for change can stay locked in your mind if you don't unlock their potential and act on them.

So let's have a real hand-holding, girlfriend heart-to-heart as I introduce you to the true-life stories in this book. My story, the one that gave a long-labor birth to this book, is in it, too. Chances are very good that you will see yourself or someone close to you experiencing the same problems with being happy as the women in the stories.

Key solutions follow each story, and using them can help change a negative life to one that is positive and happy. There are also two chapters at the end of the book with steps and positive reinforcement to help you on your search, as well as an update on the stories of each woman in the book.

We begin with a Happiness Quiz, simple questions to help you identify your true feelings about your own happiness.

Just remember, happiness is here for you. Now. You simply have to be prepared to see it and use the right keys to unlock it.

Kristen Houghton

The Happiness Quiz

Taking the Happiness Quiz will help you understand your personal ideas about happiness. There are no right answers to this quiz. No quiz in the world will automatically change your life. What it will do is make you think about changing and decide how you might want to go about doing that. The best way to use this or any quiz is to be completely open about your feelings. The quiz helps you discover who you are and in what direction you are headed in your quest for that elusive state called happiness.

While this quiz may light a spark of change in you, nothing happens overnight. Do you have a negative personality, a bad relationship, a lifestyle you want changed? It always takes time to make necessary changes, but it can be done and will be done if you decide to take charge. After you finish reading the true stories of women just like you and understand the keys and the solutions to the problems presented, you may want to return to this quiz and review your answers. Your own ideas may have changed or may be in the process of changing, and you will view happiness in a different way.

Don't Think about Being Happy Tomorrow!

Remember Margaret Mitchell's heroine, Scarlett O'Hara, and her favorite saying, *"I won't think about it now. I'll think about it tomorrow"*?

She used that saying as a way of blocking out what she didn't want to face at the moment. The attitudes of her modern counterparts haven't changed all that much! We can't face the idea of happiness for one reason or another and so, "We'll think about being happy tomorrow!" It is procrastination in its most basic form.

Women have been sabotaging themselves for a long time by making happiness an almost unattainable goal. By placing something in the future, you are unconsciously saying that you don't have to worry or think about it now. But you do. If you postpone being happy, your past, present, and future will be exactly the same: empty and unfulfilled.

The questions in the following quiz have been designed to help you decide your personal happiness level at the present time. Be honest with yourself as you read and answer them. They are straightforward, no-nonsense questions. Apply them to your own unique situation.

No self-delusion, no untruths, no one to see how you really feel except you. There's no gain in cheating—you'll only cheat yourself. It won't be graded. You're the only one who will see it.

Ready?
Let's go!

Assessing Your personal Happiness— Is It Your Priority?*

1. How do you wake up in the morning? Do you dread the day ahead every day?

2. Are you always last on your to-do list?

3. How would you like to direct your energy and time to fulfill your life?

4. Who or what strongly influences how you live your life?

5. Can you reinvent yourself when your life is not going the way you planned or takes an unpleasant unexpected turn?

6. Do you have happy memories of your past?

7. If you are in an unhappy no-win relationship, are you willing and able to walk away no matter how difficult it may be?

8. Finish this statement: "The way I am living right now makes me feel..."

9. Where do you feel the most comfortable during the day?

10. Do you readily allow your personal goals to always be postponed for other people?

11. How do you really feel about yourself? Be honest.

*Answers are in chapter 13.

12. If you could magically go back ten years, what would you do differently?

13. At what age do you feel that it's too late for you to begin a dream?

14. Finish this statement: "Before I can be happy, I need . . ."

15. What is your definition of being wealthy?

16. What would you change about your life?

17. Do you think other people are happier than you? Why?

18. If you were happy, how would you act differently?

19. What is your emotional style when things don't go according to your plans?

20. What can you do to be happy right now and in the future?

You've taken the quiz and been completely honest. You know that you're not really happy. In chapter 13 you will find key advice for your personal answers. Though no answer you give is wrong, these keys will give you added insight in why you may be "just this side" of the State of Happiness.

Are you ready to help yourself to make changes? Good. Let's get started by reading the true stories of women just like you and me.

CHAPTER 1

The Key to Relationships
Never Let Any One Person Be in Charge of Your Happiness

Do you believe that someone else can provide happiness for you? If you do, you're not alone. Too many women go into relationships believing that the men they love will automatically be able to *make* them happy.

Believing this fairy tale is one of the most emotionally costly mistakes you can make. No one can make you happy, and you should not assign that job to anyone but you. The ability to be happy falls squarely on your shoulders. Depending on someone else for your own joy will leave you constantly disappointed and frustrated.

In rural parts of India, there is a blessing that a mother gives to her daughter on the eve of the daughter's wedding. Holding her daughter's hand between her own two, the mother says:

"My daughter, never let any one person be in charge of your happiness."

It is good advice, subtly stating that a woman should *not* depend upon her husband for her happiness. The bride-to-be understands that she needs to seek, and find, her own happiness wherever it may be.

It would have been good advice for our first happiness seeker, Debora.

DEBORA'S STORY

Debora was an economic analyst and an accomplished amateur painter. She was well liked by her colleagues, had a nice town house, enjoyed a circle of good friends, and was financially in a good place. Her job was a dream where she met with midlevel men and women in government, and she carried it off admirably and easily. Debora was fortunate to work with people who were not only professionals but genuinely caring individuals.

By all accounts she was on the way to a solid, long-term career in her chosen profession, and she could look forward to many years of doing the work she loved. As for her artwork, some of her watercolors—which had won awards in small art exhibits—hung on the wall of her office. Life could have been very sweet.

But Debora was not happy. Her unhappiness sprang from an unsatisfying relationship with Rob.

They had been together for over five years, and while Debora was more than willing to set a marriage date, Rob was totally against it. He was a taciturn man, lacking in compassion, who was more a taker than a giver in their relationship. He came and went at will without problem and rarely paid any household expenses. In fact, the only item he had brought with him when he moved in with Debora was an inexpensive cappuccino machine that never worked properly; it was capable of producing only lukewarm coffee, which was a pretty good description of Rob's emotions for Debora as well.

He was also very critical and mocking of any and all of Debora's accomplishments. As far as he was concerned, her watercolors were "ridiculous dabs of paint," and he told her she spent way too much effort and time painting "nothing that will ever sell." To appease him, Debora did her painting when he wasn't around and hid her finished artwork in the basement.

She began avoiding friends whom Rob disliked, and she stopped talking about work because he told her that, quite frankly, it bored him.

She even put up with him calling her Debs, a nickname she hated. Debora was willing to do anything for Rob, even to the point of making changes that left her uncomfortable.

Debora placed all her conditions for happiness squarely on the weak shoulders of Rob and because of this was continually disappointed. She began thinking of her life in the future tense.

"When Rob tells me he loves me, then I'll be happy."

"As we're together longer, I know he'll become more understanding and kinder, and then I'll be happy."

"When Rob changes his mind about marriage, *then* I'll be happy!"

While waiting for the future to come so she *could* be happy, she wasted her present. Rob was not going to change his attitude about marriage. He told her from the very beginning of their relationship that marriage with her was just not going to happen. There was no chance that he was going to become a "kinder, more understanding person" and say he loved her. Rob was who he was and Debora's hopes for the future were nothing more than hopes, without substance.

She was doomed to be unhappy because she wasted her potential for happiness while waiting for Rob to be the man she wanted. Simple things that *could* have made her happy, like friendship, her artistic talent, and her profession, all became insignificant. She continuously waited for the right conditions for happiness, and those conditions absolutely *had* to include a "nicer" version of Rob.

Debora went so far as to seek the counsel of a relationship therapist, where she complained about how her happiness was being put on hold *because* of Rob. She ranted and raved that Rob was keeping her from being a happy person. In tears she told the therapist that if only *Rob* would change, her life would be perfect. When her therapist suggested that Rob might *never* commit to a permanent relationship such as marriage, Debora vehemently disagreed. She truly believed that he would eventually change his mind and they would marry.

The therapist then told her Rob was *not* responsible for making her happy, that only she, Debora, could be in charge of her own happiness. Perhaps she would be better off *without* Rob, who seemed to be a callous and very critical person. Debora was shocked.

"But I can't be happy *without* Rob! If only he'd change, then I would be the happiest person in the world! It's him, not me!" she cried.

Eventually she left therapy because, as she said, "It just wasn't working."

Blinded and Blindsided

They had been together for almost seven years when Debora came home early from a business trip and found Rob putting boxes of his personal items into his car.

"You came back early," he said. His tone was so accusing that Debora almost felt as if she should apologize for showing up at her own home. Then, with a sinking feeling, she asked him what he was doing.

"I'm moving out," he said. "I left you an e-mail."

Debora just stared at him in utter shock. Angry at her disbelieving look, Rob continued, "Come on, Debs! You should have seen this coming. You knew our relationship was going nowhere. I've changed, you haven't, and I want a new life."

Actually, Debora really *was* blindsided by this statement, because she simply had not been aware of any major changes in Rob. He was as he always had been: secretive, aloof, and anti-commitment. As for lack of changes in her, why hadn't he *told* her what he wanted from her? She would have been more than happy to change anything in her life for him. What was so different about their relationship now that he felt he had to move out? What new life was he talking about?

Standing on a sidewalk in front of her town house as Rob casually placed the last box into the car, she pleaded with him not to leave. With strangers passing by staring at the surreal scenario, Debora was certainly not prepared for what Rob had to tell her next. Turning to her, he delivered the final and cruelest blow to their relationship.

He'd met someone else about a year ago. He was getting married in three months. When Debora just stared at him, Rob became nasty.

"I explained all that in the e-mail I left you, for God's sake! Stop staring. You look like an idiot."

Debora said the first thing that popped into her head.

"You mean you were seeing her while you were with

me? You planned a wedding with her while you were living *here*?"

She was almost incoherent with tears and rage when Rob nonchalantly nodded yes. All she could think to say to him was, "You're marrying another woman? Not me? But why? You told me that you *never* wanted to get married!"

His reply was as callous and cold as any answer he'd ever given her. As he got into the driver's seat, he said: "No, Debs, I said I never wanted to marry *you*. But she's not like you; she's a *happy* person."

That Debora didn't try to choke Rob had a lot to do with the fact that he gunned the motor and roared down the street.

In the privacy of her living room, she read Rob's e-mail. It was curt and short. Almost like a business letter, Debora thought, impersonal and to the point, not much of an explanation at all.

I am engaged to be married and have moved out.
I've notified the post office of my new address. You
can keep the cappuccino machine, I have a new one.
This change will be good for me. Rob.

That was it, nothing more. No "sorry it didn't work out for us," no regrets, nothing. A cold note and an old cappuccino machine was all she had left from seven years of putting Rob first. That ugly old machine, which produced such horrible coffee, represented Rob and their relationship together: cold, depressing, and unable to be fixed. In a rage, Debora grabbed the machine and smashed it against the wall.

She became, in her own words, "a crazy woman." She desperately tried calling Rob at work, only to be told by the receptionist that he would no longer take her calls. E-mails she sent him were blocked. The one time she waited outside his office building to see him, a security guard walked over to her and demanded that she leave, telling her that if she persisted in "harassing the gentleman," legal action would be taken. Rob had swiftly and successfully taken himself out of her life.

Debora was devastated for almost two years after he left. Her career suffered, and she stopped painting. No longer taking care of herself, she looked ten years older than she really was. Over and over she blamed her unhappiness on Rob and made herself miserable. While Rob went on with *his* life, Debora wallowed in if-onlys, and her future became as stagnant as her past. She had reached the lowest point of her life.

Finally, a very concerned colleague convinced her to go back into therapy, and this time it worked because Debora allowed it to do so. Bitter but so much wiser after two years of therapy, she began to start a new life.

But Debora was luckier in a way than Sara; Sara *married* her Mr. Callous.

SARA'S STORY

Sara was a teacher and, like many other women, thought that after marriage she'd find happiness. She also thought that the man she was marrying would miraculously change after the wedding. To make him happy she even converted to his religion—one he himself rarely practiced.

He was moody if he didn't get his way and, while she hated to admit it, he was also selfish. Actually, her parents and several friends had tried in vain to dissuade her from marrying Brian, saying he was shallow, self-absorbed, and never satisfied. However, Sara's reply to them was that she knew him "better than he knows himself."

Her friends privately laughed at that statement. Many of them knew what a rude and annoying person Brian really was and dreaded the times when Sara brought him along to social gatherings. He had a sense of humor that bordered on cruelty, and this seemed evident to all but Sara. Her family was so concerned about her that they urged her to seriously reconsider spending a life with him.

"Brian literally runs your life. You will *not* be happy with him, Sara," her mother said.

But Sara listened to nobody.

At the wedding reception, while Sara was smiling and greeting guests, Brian looked bored and annoyed. When Sara saw this, she went over to him and tried to make him happy. The more she tried, the grumpier he became, causing the videographer to comment to Sara's father that he didn't have one happy newlywed moment recorded.

"Can't his own bride get that guy to smile?" he asked, mystified.

On their honeymoon, while other newlywed couples were hand-holding and generally happy to be starting their lives together, Brian was his usual self, causing Sara to put herself in charge of his complaint department. Very little satisfied him, and he let her know. The food was overrated, the drinks were watered down, he didn't enjoy the land or water sports, and on and on and on. The one time he actually was enjoying himself on a boating trip, Sara was so relieved she burst into tears. At the end of the two weeks, her nerves were raw.

Sara's life with Brian was sad, to say the least. It was also a hell of an emotional roller-coaster ride. On the rare occasions that he was in a good mood, Sara felt uplifted and full of hope. She also felt that she had finally done "something right" to make him happy. But when he returned to his usual nasty self, picking on Sara for anything and everything, she was plunged down to the depths of despair. Living with him wreaked havoc not only on her emotional health but on her physical well-being as well. Her husband wore her down to a nub. Finally, because she was so miserable, Sara's doctor put her on strong anti-depressants.

You Don't Need Anti-Depressants, You Need a Divorce!

Living with Brian made Sara feel as if she were carrying an enormous weight: the weight of trying to please a man who was never satisfied with anything. She was tired all the time and felt no real joy in any part of her life. One of her fifth-grade students asked her why she was so sad all the time. The sadness came from the mental fatigue of living with someone who was rarely in a pleasant mood.

When she thought about it, Sara did see that Brian was "difficult" and that perhaps, just perhaps, she shouldn't have married him hoping to change his moody demeanor. She couldn't admit this to anyone else, though. Hadn't people told her that she would be making a mistake by marrying Brian and hoping for happiness? Sara had a hard time admitting this to her own self, let alone family and friends.

And then, too, there was the anger issue. There were times when she felt filled with rage at Brian and her neverending quest to create a happy life for him. It took a great deal out of her. She saw colleagues going for post-grad degrees and moving forward with their careers. She had neither the time nor the energy to do so and she felt, deep inside, that she was stagnating in her professional life.

Sara hated to think that her marriage was a mistake. There were those rare precious moments when Brian *was* in a good mood. At those times she saw only the man whose smile and good looks had dazzled her, and it made her want to try all the harder to please him and keep him in that good mood.

Happiness isn't...

...hoping someone else will make you happy. Depending on another to provide you with happiness makes it a sure bet that you won't be happy. You are the only one who can provide happiness for yourself through your talents, lifestyle, and attitude.

Since her pride wouldn't let her talk to family or close girlfriends, Sara was desperate for someone to tell her that she had *not* made a mistake in marrying Brian and that everything would be all right sometime soon. She decided to ask for advice from a close, older confidant of hers who taught at the same school she did. As her teaching mentor, he had always given her good career advice; maybe he could help her now. He was a practical man, a father and a grandfather, and Sara respected his opinions.

They talked at lunch and after classes, and Sara told him how she was waiting for the "right time" to be happy. Intense discussions followed, with Sara doing almost all the talking. She talked about her future happiness, her supposed failings as a wife, how she felt it was *her* fault that Brian was the way he was, her husband's moodiness, and the fragile atmosphere in their home.

When she finally asked her friend why it seemed she could never succeed in making her husband happy, it brought what Sara considered an unbelievable remark from a man who had been happily married for more than thirty years.

After weeks of having listened to Sara talk about her husband, her endless efforts to make him happy to no avail, and how she couldn't *possibly* be happy unless Brian was, her friend told her,

"Maybe you shouldn't keep trying to make *him* happy, Sara. Brian might not be worth all your efforts. You might want to work on making yourself happy for a change. There is no *right* time for happiness. Happiness should be in the here and now. It is your right. We were put on earth to be happy. You don't need anti-depressants, Sara. I believe you need a divorce!"

But Sara viewed divorce as a defeat of all her efforts, and she was determined not to give up. Her here and now was spent trying to make Brian happy so that someday, when she had succeeded in doing that, *she* could finally be happy herself! Her thoughts that her marriage may have been a mistake, her anger at Brian, her isolation from family and friends—all were pushed to the side as she intensified her efforts in making her marriage work. After all, what did she have without Brian? Her happiness depended on him!

They're still married, and she's still trying to please him. And her happiness is still out of reach, somewhere in the future when Brian's own happiness will finally allow *her* to be happy. And that day will never come.

The best of relationships are complicated enough without adding unneeded pressure to the mix. You need to seriously take stock of the give-and-take situation that exists between the both of you. If it is more give than take on your part, you have to ask yourself why this is happening.

Putting the Relationship into Perspective: The Basic Keys to Owning Your Own Happiness

He needs to be a good fit for you and your life.
If this sounds cold or harsh to you, think about what your life will be with this man. Any good relationship should enhance your life as a person. You should both be secure in common ideas. If commitment is high on your agenda, it makes no sense to be with someone who is commitment-phobic.

The relationship should be a good mix of common ground and new experiences. Life together should be a pleasure, not a second job.

You need support for your wants and needs, too.
To ensure a future of happiness, your goals need to be addressed. Being supportive, being loving should never be one-sided; it should be a mutual part of any relationship. You cannot always be the giver and receive nothing in return. Constantly giving to an unappreciative someone else makes you see your own life as insignificant. If

he mocks your goals or minimizes your achievements, seriously rethink staying in the relationship.

He isn't worth it.

Define the real you.

What makes you tick, what special talents do you possess; who is the real you? These may sound very much like those ridiculous questions your high school guidance counselor might have asked you in order to determine "what you should do in life," but the answers are important. You need to know who you are and who you're going to be before you can begin to be part of a couple. The two halves of that whole, the couple, should complement each other. There has to be a "me" in the "we."

Be realistic instead of romantic.

See the person with whom you want to share your life, your bed—your *bathroom,* for heaven's sake!—for who he really is and not who you *want* him to be. He doesn't have to be perfect—even Brad Pitt has his flaws—but as a whole package he should be someone you like and who likes you.

Yes, you read that right—*like.* Liking the person, not just loving him, is the key basis for a workable and solid relationship. Liking makes loving strong and durable.

In the simplest terms, view a potential relationship from a "liking" point of view. In life there are people with whom you'd like to enjoy a leisurely gourmet meal and then there are those with whom you wouldn't even want to have a quick cup of coffee! Give yourself a reality check when it comes to love. Is he worth a gourmet meal? If you decide he isn't, he is not for you.

Live your life within and without the relationship.
This is your life, too. You are an individual. Although shar-
ing time and activities together can be wonderful, doing
something apart from the relationship is crucial to your
growth and sanity. Don't give up what is important to you
as a person simply to please another. Giving up any part of
what makes you "you" is giving up too much.

Before you commit to any relationship, you must learn
to be alone and love yourself. This may seem a simple
thing to do, but it isn't. The media is filled with images
of romantic couples, and you are made to feel something
is not right with you if you aren't part of a couple. While
loving and being loved is one of the most wonderful experiences that can happen to you, you need to own your life
before you merge with another.

RELATIONSHIPS 101: LESSONS LEARNED

You may never be able to change the man in your relationship, but there is a great deal you can do to change
you. Take responsibility for your own happiness. You
place a tremendous burden on another person by asking
that he provide you with the intangible gift of happiness.
Even the best and most loving of people will have a hard
time providing that gift on a daily basis!

Expecting happiness to automatically come from others will leave you waiting, wanting, and frustrated.

If Debora had first tried to make herself happy, taking joy in her friendships, her profession, and her art, she
may have seen that the only area of her life that wasn't
working was her relationship with Rob. To be happy, *she*
would have left *him!*

Sara made a mistake in marrying a person whom she already *knew* was selfish and moody. She chose to close her eyes to what was right there in front of her! Unfortunately, Sara bought into her belief in "wedded bliss" and the myth that marriage will change an unpleasant, selfish person into a sweet-natured, loving spouse. But a snarling pit bull will never become Lassie.

Both Debora and Sara were on a fool's errand. The only people who changed, and not in a positive way, were they themselves. They became sad, depressed, angry women trying over and over again to fix a bad situation, only to get the same results.

Though both women sought advice for their problems—Debora went to a professional, Sara to her mentor—no positive changes could be made until each woman was willing to do so. Debora's decision to change, though eventually very good for her, came about through a miserable breakup. She had no choice but to do something to help herself. Sara has yet to change and may never take the action necessary to begin a new life. She sees divorce as "giving up" and until she can change that mind-set, she can't change anything else.

Choices are individual, and no one action is right for every person, but one thing is crystal clear: You need to value your own life. Make yourself happy and you will become a person with the ability to enhance happiness in others. Ownership of personal happiness is the key ingredient for any healthy relationship.

Unhappily Ever After Is Not an Option

Both Debora and Sara made a mistake in not personally taking charge of their own lives. They stopped living in reality and existed in a world that had nothing to do with their own hopes and dreams. Neither one realized that the responsibility for happiness lay within her grasp. Too much time was wasted in fruitless relationships and unrealistic hopes.

Avoiding this type of "living" is necessary to having a healthy life. We are too often blinded to reality. Whether it is ego or having seen too many Disney movies with happy endings as a little girl, a woman waits for her prince to arrive bringing with him all the happiness she will ever need.

But real life is not like movies. There are no scriptwriters creating perfect and satisfying endings. Debora and Sara were attracted to men who, all too obviously to other observers in their lives, did not love them and used them for their own selfish needs.

There are lines in romance novels that perfectly sum up the mind-set of women like Debora and Sara. Phrases like:

"She knew immediately that she would sacrifice *anything* to spend her life with this *man*. He was her happiness."

"Like so many women before her, she was willing to give up everything to be with him; her family, her future, her own happiness . . . When *he* was happy, she would be happy *through* him . . ."

"*He* was her world! Without him she had nothing."

They make nice love stories, but in reality, it never works. You, and only you, are responsible for our own happiness, and that is as it should be.

CHAPTER 2

⚷ The Key to Avoiding Being a Have-Not
To Have and Have Not Isn't Just the Title of an Old Movie

How do you define what a good, satisfying life is for yourself? How do you see success in a career or in financial terms as it relates to you personally? Everyone has a different image of what successful means. You may be influenced by the media or what society tells you. Or experience may have taught you that success is attained only after certain conditions have been satisfied. Whatever your own personal idea of success is, you may find *your* story in the stories of Belinda and Elise. Each one defined the state of personal success very differently, and each woman was never satisfied.

BELINDA'S STORY
Belinda was fond of saying that if it weren't for bad luck, she'd have no luck at all. Her definition of being lucky and successful was having money. Lots of it.

"You're not successful if you don't have a lot of money. I don't want to be one of have-nots in life! That's like having no luck at all."

Actually, as far as success and luck go, most people would consider Belinda to have had both. She and her family were healthy, they did not live in poverty, she and her husband had good jobs, and their kids didn't give them any more trouble than the normal childhood problems. But Belinda wanted more.

When a friend told her she should count her blessings, Belinda responded by pointing out that a mutual acquaintance had so much more.

"But," her friend countered, "she and her husband are at their wits' end because their son has a drug problem! You *are* lucky that you don't have *that* misery, don't you think?"

Belinda didn't see it that way.

"At least they have more *money*. Listen, their son might have a drug problem, but look at the rehab center they can send him to! You've got to have *big* bucks for that! I'd never be able to afford that place. My kids would end up in some horrible state-run facility."

She was adamant in her beliefs.

"They are the haves in this world and my husband and I are the have-nots. I don't have enough *money* to be happy yet. If Bill and I could just win the lottery, I know I'd be happy! Money buys happiness. Until then . . ."

Belinda had had a childhood where money was never discussed but where every cent was accounted for in minute detail. Her parents looked for sales and usually bought no-name brands. Nothing was quality in their home.

There were no delicate crystal glasses to drink from; the glasses in Belinda's home were cheap plastic tumblers for the adults and empty jelly and marmalade jars for the kids. Their dishes were from some yard sale. It bothered her that her mother didn't seem to care that she was a have-not. Items that were not quality but considered good enough by her parents always seemed to keep her one step away from having what the other girls had, and it hurt.

When Belinda was eleven, she asked for a specific pair of sneakers for her birthday. These sneakers were tremendously popular among her classmates. They were white with pink sparkles that would shine in the dark. The pink laces had real heart-shaped crystals at the tips; they even had a secret pocket on the side that was zipped by a tiny bell. How she wanted to be one of those girls who made that faint ringing sound when she walked!

Two days before her birthday, while putting towels away in the linen closet, Belinda saw a large shoe box tied with ribbons and a card that had her name on it. She was thrilled! *Finally* she was going to have something the other girls had.

The day of her birthday, she smiled over the home-made cake her mother brought to the table. She knew other girls always had a nicer one bought at the pastry shop, but what's a cake? After all, she was now going to actually have something all the others had.

Belinda smiled through the presentation of a stick drawing her little brother gave her, a cheap watch sent by her grandfather, underwear from a maiden aunt, and waited for the only present that really mattered.

But as soon as she opened the prettily decorated box, her heart sank and she felt tears come to her eyes. The box held a plain white pair of sneakers, no sparkles, no crystals. The fact that her father gave her a pair of bells to slip through the laces only made it worse.

Belinda never wore the sneakers.

Caviar Dreams, Tuna Fish Budget: Lifestyle of a Rich Wannabe

Thus began a lifelong affliction called envy. Belinda was jealous of anyone who had money. Even though she knew nothing about their private lives or any heartbreak others may have suffered, she knew they had money, and that was enough for her to dislike them.

She took out heavy loans for college and became a credit card junkie just so she could have what other students had and do what they did. It took her a trip to a credit counselor and six full years to pay off the credit card debt. Her credit rating was severely damaged.

Happiness isn't . . .

. . . only money and material possessions.

Please note the word *only*. While there is absolutely nothing wrong with having the best of everything, this should not be a be-all and end-all for happiness. Money can buy you happiness if it is used to purchase or support a dream or a goal. Living comfortably and to your taste is good for you.

She met Bill, who had a bright future and was distantly related to a wealthy family. Unfortunately for Belinda, a distant relative was all he ever was. After marriage, like the fictional title character in Gustave Flaubert's *Madame Bovary,* what Belinda did have was never good enough. She read magazines that showed beautiful, expensive furniture and when she compared it with hers, she felt discouraged. How could she have people in her house when her furniture was "junk"? She devoured catalogs from high-end fashion stores and felt unattractive when she and Bill went out because she didn't have "the right clothes."

Every thought she had of perfection was placed in the future when, by some miracle, she would have money.

A vacation to the Bahamas was nothing because people she knew were going to Europe. A remodeled kitchen wasn't good enough since it hadn't been remodeled by a decorator. Other people had decorators.

She used her energy and time to think of ways to live the lifestyle she felt she should have. Once, late at night, sleepless and unhappy, she saw a commercial for a home equity loan. Belinda quickly calculated how much equity was in their house and thought of all she could have with the money.

When she told her husband what she wanted to do, he refused to even consider such an action, telling her it would only create money trouble down the road. He'd slowly paid off the debt she'd accrued on his credit cards and her delinquent student loans until he was finally able to start saving some money.

The last thing they wanted, he told her, was to be in debt again.

"Please, Belinda, we have enough to live a comfortable life. Let's not put ourselves in debt."

She had come a long way from her penny-pinching childhood, but Belinda would never be satisfied with just being comfortable.

Not only did Belinda put her own happiness on hold, she didn't see the happiness in the day-to-day life of her family—and because she didn't see it, she didn't participate in it. She missed out on a great deal. Her children's Little

League games and school plays, her husband being honored at a banquet his company held for yearly achievements, her daughter winning first prize in debate; none of that mattered to her. Her family sensed that she was unhappy, and it was contagious. They became dissatisfied with their own lives. People began to avoid Belinda because, as one friend said, "Her whole body oozes depression."

Belinda was always looking to some future date for her happiness, "when we have money," and, of course, it wasn't happening. But what a waste of life! She took no joy in the present, saw the past as a failure, and waited for a money-filled future that wasn't coming. Family moments were marred because she thought others had more than she did. She literally lived through her fantasy of what she would do and how she would feel when she had "enough money to buy happiness."

It is hard to live every day yearning for a life that you don't have. Envy of what others *have*, and the frustration of what you *don't*, build to boiling points. You are in a constant state of misery.

•••

Calling yourself a have-not isn't limited just to not having money. Some people equate being a have-not with having the right kind of success or not. Elise, in the next story, is the perfect example of an "unsuccessful" success.

ELISE'S STORY

Elise bought into the Madison Avenue idea of what a successful woman should be. She had set her sights for happiness in the distant future. Ever since childhood, she had dreamed of becoming a fashion designer, and her dream was encouraged by the single mother who had raised her.

Mom was a successful woman in her own right, having gone back to college after a messy divorce and eventually doing something she thoroughly enjoyed. She owned her own real estate business. A small business, nothing major, but she was happy.

Encouraging her daughter in her dream, her mother often quoted the famous line, "Do what you truly love, Elise, success will certainly follow."

The fact that Elise had a dream to pursue was good for her. She knew what she wanted and made plans at a young age to achieve that goal. When others didn't quite know what they were going to do after high school, Elise was confident and resolute in her choice. Her dream would bring her fame.

Coming of age in a time when women were becoming more prominent in the corporate world, Elise held the belief that was presented via the media, and society, to women of her generation. Commercials, advertisements, and the news subtly (and sometimes not so subtly) conveyed that you could only call yourself successful if you reached the highest pinnacle of your profession. The message was clear: Women not only *could* have it all, they definitely *should*.

Happiness depended on absolute 100 percent success; nothing else would do.

Elise felt that only by becoming a famous couturier would she be considered successful. At that time she would be respected, sought after, and, most of all, happy. She clung to her dream like a lifesaver on a stormy sea.

Worldwide fame was the only way she could be happy. Wasn't that the message of the day?

"When I . . . and then I'll . . ." became a sort of mantra for Elise as she diligently worked through design school while holding down various temp jobs. It was difficult and exhausting, and she had no social life at all, but she comforted herself with thoughts of future success as an international designer. Happiness was a few years away.

After graduating from Parsons School of Design, she worked a few years for small fashion houses. Nights and weekends were spent designing her own clothing line. When she showed a few handmade outfits to one of her employers, he agreed to put them on display. The designs were that good.

Happiness isn't . . .

. . . an unrealistic idea of success and discounting what you have achieved as not good enough. Celebrate your success each step of the way.

Very soon she was selling her one-of-a-kind designs to women in society. She opened a small boutique in New York and did quite well. Well enough, in fact, to open another shop in Palm Beach, Florida. Her mother was proud of her.

She met and then married an intelligent man who owned an upscale restaurant in Chelsea. Their combined incomes gave them a glamorous lifestyle that included the freedom for frequent travel and lavish parties.

It seemed to everyone that all of her dedication had paid off. Elise had a prosperous business and traveled the world with an equally successful husband.

So was Elise happy? Not at all.

That she has a good marriage, financial security, and a fair share of success in her chosen field is not enough. Anyone else looking at her would see a successful person. It is sad that the only person who really mattered, Elise herself, minimized her achievements.

You develop a relationship with certain ideas you have about success. But success, whether it involves money or renown, doesn't have to meet only one specific standard. You need to define success as it relates to your situation. There are five essential keys you can use to measure personal success.

HOW TO STOP THINKING YOU ARE A HAVE-NOT: THE KEYS TO PERSONAL SUCCESS AND FULFILLMENT

Understand that success and reality go hand in hand.

If beauty is in the eye of the beholder, then beauty's cousin, success, is in an individual's personal perception. Why should anyone dictate what success is for you? Success is subjective. You need to identify your own idea of success, *not* that of someone else. When you have done that, couple it with a healthy dose of reality in what you can achieve.

Both Belinda and Elise had pretty good lives, and both failed to realize it. Each one had set-in-stone prerequisites for happiness that could not be met and were self-defeating.

Have a backup plan and a secondary goal.

One of the best pieces of advice about success I have ever heard came from an actor friend. He talked about the importance of having a backup plan for his professional goals. Both parts of his plan for success had to do with the theater.

"I fully intend to make it as an actor on Broadway, but I also have a secondary goal. I want to direct plays. That's my plan B just in case. Who knows? At some point I may decide that directing is more fulfilling. I want to give myself options."

Knowing that there is something you can fall back on, a plan B, eliminates stress and the fear of failure. Having more options gives you more chances for success and happiness.

Celebrate your levels of success.

A person who runs a thriving business is certainly not on the level of a Donald Trump—but can that person still be called successful? Yes! Is someone who enjoys fame on Broadway as successful as a Hollywood actor who makes millions per picture? Absolutely! It is all in the mind of the person.

You don't have to live on the same scale as someone else. Celebrate you for what you have achieved. See yourself as a success and find contentment in what you have now.

Make it a rule to see yourself as a unique person with unique talents. No one else is you. Don't focus on what *they* have or how successful *they* are. They should not hold the highest importance in your life. Instead, focus on the one person who should be important to you—your own self.

Rethink the idea of nothing less than 100 percent.
If you have made it a point of honor that you can only be happy when everything goes exactly the way you want it to go, then you are setting yourself up for disappointment. Let go of that attitude now! This way of thinking can only become a negative trap.

Find a satisfactory medium in your life so you can enjoy what's there in front of you. An all-or-nothing attitude is a sure way of guaranteeing that you end up with nothing.

Know your own value.
Don't become a victim of envy. Stop thinking about what you don't have and focus instead on what you do have at this moment. Understand that feeling good about what you have in no way makes you complacent. You are not settling for less, you are simply enjoying the now part of your life.

Make a list of your talents and what you think is great about you. Sell yourself to *you*. This isn't being vain or narcissistic; it's discovering what your real value is. It is not only productive but will also have a positive effect on how you perceive yourself.

Reinvent yourself, make changes as you go along, but understand that you are living your life and not that of someone else. Your mind controls how you see the world around you. You become what you think you are.

A SUCCESSFUL LIFE REINTERPRETED 101: LESSONS LEARNED

Being someone with a dream is a good thing. It can only turn bad when the dream becomes distorted. If you are never satisfied with the goal you reach, all your success seems worthless to you. The balance between being successful and actually enjoying that success is disrupted.

Nothing can make you as miserable as always being envious of what others have. It manifests itself in emotional and physical discomfort. Instead of walking in the sunlight, envious people hide in dark corners.

Headaches and sleeplessness come from negative emotions and thoughts. Envy becomes an insidious disease eventually affecting your ability to do anything positive. Certainly the person who constantly bemoans the fact that "everyone else has so much more than I do" defeats her motivation to take the actions that would change her lifestyle. Take the energy you expend on complaining about what you *don't* have and shift it to improving your lifestyle and getting what you *do* want.

Don't set yourself up for failure by believing that there is only one real measure of success and anything less is unacceptable. You are punishing yourself by believing this. Never stop trying to improve yourself, but take some joy during the process.

The wildly successful and the fabulously wealthy will always be curiosities in our society. It is human nature. They may be different from you and me, but that doesn't mean there is happiness for them. If you research the lives of people who have become successful or have made a fortune, many times you will find stories of sadness to go along with the acclaim.

Belinda lost the joy of her children's childhood and moments of marital contentment because she was never satisfied. Every occasion when she could have found happiness was marred due to the feeling that she couldn't be happy *because* . . .

If material items are important (and as we know, there is absolutely nothing wrong with being a woman who enjoys quality possessions), then go after them—but do so in a reasonable, realistic manner. While you're going after what your future wants, though, don't miss out on your today.

Belinda put herself in debt to have what others had. When she could no longer use credit to have what she desired, she became a miserable and unhappy person. She enjoyed nothing.

While you may envy what other people have and desire more material things in your life, spending time brooding about what you don't have feeds the "envy monster." The bigger it grows, the more it consumes your life and the less you live.

Are you looking for success? That's great. Don't forget to celebrate *all* of your achievements toward your goal, even the small ones. Success comes in varying degrees and should really be defined by how much you *enjoy* what you do. If you can make a living doing something you enjoy, wonderful!

Elise gave up a lot while pursuing her dream, but her idea of success hinged on being a world-renowned designer. The fact that a select group of wealthy patrons came to her for personally designed outfits didn't mean she was successful, at least not in her mind. She let generic messages from the media and society decree what her success *should* be.

She had success but, since it wasn't her idea of success, she denied herself any chance of happiness she might have derived from it. The precise standards she sets for her exclusive outfits are the same ones she sets for her happiness. *Everything* must be perfect, and the price is high. But what she doesn't realize is that while her designs are made of expensive materials and are quite costly, happiness is free.

She still keeps thinking that if she could only get to be recognized globally, she would be happy. She keeps asking herself, "I did what I loved—where's my success?" Elise is still waiting for her future dream to bring her happiness.

Intelligent and sophisticated as she is, the idea that she would allow anyone or anything to define personal success and happiness seems almost ridiculous. No one tells her how to run her business or how to design an outfit. She would never allow that. Yet she follows the criteria created by others for when she can be happy. It is unfortunate that we can be so heavily influenced by what "they" (whoever "they" are) tell us, but even the savviest woman in charge of a major company permits this to happen at times.

Not feeling worthy and not allowing yourself to enjoy what you already have is an unfortunate attitude that gets you nowhere and has a long-lasting effect on your outlook. You are worthy of happiness simply because you exist, but you don't realize it. How you find your happiness is entirely up to you. You need to focus on unlocking negative chains and actions that keep you from being happy.

So many women wear chains they've created and put on themselves. Somehow we've forgotten how to use the key we already have in our possession. Using the key is crucial to freeing yourself and discovering that the prospect of happiness has been freed along with you.

You can live almost your entire life "locked" in a mindset that prevents you from being happy. Waiting for happiness makes you a prisoner with your own negative habits and thoughts as your jailers. You absentmindedly forget where you put the damn key! Who dictates what success is for you? Do *you* decide your personal success or do you buy into what others think it should be? Why would you define *your* success by someone else's standard? Think seriously before you answer. If you are basing success on the ideas of another and not your own, you will never be truly successful. You will only see happiness in the future tense and never in the present.

The key to being successful is seeing it in increments and celebrating each step no matter how small. Don't stop *reaching* for the stars, but appreciate what you *do* have and all you've accomplished at the *present* time.

As for the negative thought that you "have nothing," be careful of what you believe. Living your life believing you're a have-not can become a self-fulfilling destiny— because eventually what you *have-not* is happiness.

CHAPTER 3

The Key to Good Parenting
Crumbs from Caesar's Table—
A Mommy Tale

There is a fantastic scene in the movie *Mildred Pierce*. Joan Crawford, as the title character, won a well-deserved Oscar for her portrayal of the loving mother who has worked and sacrificed all her life for her self-centered daughter, Vida. Finally the daughter asks her mother to make the ultimate sacrifice. Vida has just committed murder and begs Mildred to take the blame for it!

In this poignant scene, which more than likely clinched the gold statuette for Ms. Crawford, her character, Mildred, goes to the police station to confess "her" crime and make one more "loving maternal sacrifice" for her selfish, conniving daughter. It is high drama indeed. I remember seeing this movie on TV one rainy summer day with my cousin. We were both thirteen years old. During the movie, my cousin turned to me and said, "Wow, what a great mom! She'll do anything for her kid!"

I, on the other hand, thought she did *way* too much for that brat, Vida!

The word *Mom* shouldn't be synonymous with the word *sacrifice,* yet that is a common modern connection. Think of terms such as sports mom, class mom, stay-at-home mom—all exalt motherhood, but all expect some type of sacrifice.

The reality of sacrificing your all for your children, while good movie material, is another way of putting your happiness somewhere in the future. It is the same as trying to survive on crumbs from a feast for which you not only bought and prepared all the food but served it to other people.

While those people were enjoying all the bounty you gave them and all the hard work you did to prepare it, you willingly accepted the crumbs left over from their plates!

But . . . how long can you live on crumbs?

Take the story of Michelle, the consummate mother who was willing to settle for crumbs from her children's lives and did not live the life she wanted for herself until it was almost too late.

MICHELLE'S STORY

Michelle was a graphic designer, a single mother, whose schedule surrounding her kids' activities was the schedule from hell. Her two kids were involved in every childhood activity you can imagine. The term *sports mom* doesn't even come close to describing all she did. Her daughter took classes in dance, gymnastics, and art, and participated in swimming, softball, and soccer. Her son played lacrosse, baseball, and hockey, and took lessons in golf and piano.

Michelle lived for her children. Besides the enormous amount of time spent ferrying them to all their activities, there was the money issue. Basically she worked simply to give them everything they wanted. She was the first to tell you that she never saw a dime from her paycheck. Besides spending money for all their lessons and activities, she also paid a killer tuition for their pricey private school. She hadn't been on a vacation or out to dinner for over six years because there simply wasn't any money left over for her.

Michelle had been a budding mezzosoprano and had harbored aspirations of becoming an opera singer. Once delighting in taking voice lessons where her teacher had told her she had real potential, she sang in productions at her college. Even after marriage and motherhood, Michelle had continued singing light opera with small theater groups and going on auditions.

But her divorce put an end to her just-started singing career. Alone and feeling guilty for divorcing their father, Michelle felt that she had to "make it up" to her children. Instead of bringing them to a therapist to help them deal with the fact that their father wanted virtually no contact with them, she used her own brand of therapy: She gave them *everything* and *anything* they wanted.

She had abandoned going on auditions because "that would mean taking time and energy away from my children." It was doubly sad because Michelle had a secret: She had been offered a position in a local opera company. She had reluctantly turned it down because the pay was low and, when the opera season was in full swing, she would have had to work nights and weekends. That she wouldn't do. She couldn't be selfish; she had to be there for her kids. Michelle was willing to do what was necessary to make up to them for not having a father in their lives.

When friends told her she should treat herself just a little, she always said: "The kids deserve the best. Someday I'll have time for myself, I'll go back to taking voice lessons and going on auditions. But that's in the future. I'm willing to sacrifice my own happiness for now."

Problem? What Michelle was doing was dead wrong not only for her but also for her kids. She used her time, energy, and resources trying to give her children "all the things to make them happy." In doing so, she had nothing left for her own life. She, like many mothers, became the sacrificial lamb. Her idea that she'd do the things she loved in the future was a way of putting off happiness. Sacrificing for her kids became habitual and addictive.

The Unimportant Life Examined

As Michelle's children got older, they *expected* to be given whatever they wanted. They became adept at manipulating their mother into giving in to their demands. If they vaguely remembered her operatic ambition at all, they thought of it as something that would stand in the way of what they wanted. In short, her children became greedy little brats created by Mom.

Michelle worked and gave; that was her life. She listened to the arias in operas by Verdi and Puccini and longed for the time when she could again indulge her passion. Somewhere in the future, of course.

Private school tuition was bad enough, but the biggest expenses were yet to come. Because they had been handed everything by their mother no matter what their behavior was like or how bad their grades were, her children slacked off in their role as students. Their social lives were their priority. After all, unlike Mom, they *had* very active social lives. So what if their grades weren't good enough to help them receive any scholarships to the universities of their choices? Mom would foot the bill; she always did.

And they were absolutely right.

Not only did Michelle take out loans to pay for their academics, she also paid for dorms, clothes, and gave them credit card accounts—which, of course, she paid. This required doing freelance work at night after having already spent a full day at her primary job.

College, graduate school, and hefty monetary gifts when they graduated, "to help them get started," had depleted Michelle financially and physically, but the sacrificing was nowhere near over. Michelle's present was just like her past, and her future looked as if it would be the same. Even now that her kids were grown and out of the house, she still thought of herself last. Satisfying their demands had become second nature to her.

Instead of seeing her as a wonderful woman who sacrificed a lot to provide them with good schools and expensive lessons for extracurricular activities, they saw her as a person who didn't matter, a woman whose sole purpose in life was to serve them. As far as they were concerned, she had no rights, and they treated her the way they saw her treat herself: as someone completely unimportant.

Michelle expected nothing from them, and that is exactly what she got. At the age of fifty-seven, she found herself living alone, with little contact from her children, except of course when they wanted something from her. They seldom visited her because, as they told her, their lives were so full and busy. If she called them, she inevitably got their voice mail. She was tired, unfulfilled in her life, and at loose ends.

Working late one night on a Web site for a company that sold posters, she came across a Buddhist proverb that had caught her attention.

In life, remember—it is better to begin in the evening than not at all.

That simple sentence made an impact on her. Michelle read it as a reminder that her life wasn't over and that she could still pursue a dream long postponed. She sat at her computer and cried. There were tears of relief that there was still a chance for a career, mingled with tears of sadness for having postponed the chance for so very long.

The next morning began what Michelle calls her "beginning": She bought a ticket for the first live opera performance she had seen in twenty years. At the performance she heard someone mention that the opera company would be holding auditions in a few weeks for a spring production. She went home and took out her old voice books, practicing every night.

A month later, nervous but with a what-do-I-have-to-lose attitude, she auditioned for a minor role in an operetta and, to her immense surprise, got the part. She told the director how she had always longed to go back to opera and was sorry that she had waited until her late fifties to do so. The woman smiled and said she hoped Michelle would become a member of the company.

"You did it now and now is what counts, not the past or the future."

Michelle continued with her auditions, getting one small part after another. When she was asked to join the company, she was elated. The salary she would receive, though nothing like the one from her work as a graphic artist, would be sufficient for her personal needs. She had finally gone back to what made her feel fulfilled and happy.

Her children were stunned. When they heard that she had quit her job and was now with the opera company full-time, they couldn't believe she had made "such a stupid move." Because she had never spoken to them about how much her goals and needs meant to her, they had no idea she had harbored such a desire. When they tried calling her, they were surprised to get *her* voice mail. Mom was the busy one now.

Were they supportive of their mother's dream? Absolutely not. But Michelle had reached a point where she had nothing left to give them, not even money, and that was a good thing. A little late, she had finally realized that it was now or never for her dream, so at the age of fifty-seven she took a chance. She had become the woman she was meant to be. Her only regret is that she hadn't balanced her life more evenly. She now feels that her children should have known that she, the same as anyone else, was entitled to certain things in life. Her focus should not have been solely on her children's lives to the detriment of her own.

While we all willingly make some type of sacrifice in life for the ones we love, especially our children, letting anyone believe that we're alive simply to supply them with everything they want diminishes us not only in their eyes but in our own. When we treat ourselves as a person of no value, so do others, including our children.

•••

The next mommy tale is slightly different than Michelle's in the area of sacrifice. You see, this mother didn't live *for* her child, she lived *through* him.

JANET'S STORY

In her most bitter moments, Janet liked to quote Shakespeare's famous line from *King Lear:* "How sharper than a serpent's tooth it is to have a thankless child!"

The fact that Janet created her "thankless child" by being the "perfect mom" made it worse.

Janet was a woman who had never really been comfortable being the center of attention. Rather than being the star, she was the type of person who saw her life's role as the star's personal assistant. School plays saw her as the one who helped out behind the scenes, running lines, making costumes. At sporting events she did the statistics and ran errands for the coaches and players. In short, she was there to make sure that other people looked good. Janet was happy to bask in the reflected glory of others who needed her. It was the same way with motherhood.

She saw her life's goal clearly: She was a mother. Her life revolved around her son from the moment of conception. She was determined that he would know how much she had sacrificed for him and so planned her happiness around her child's future success. He would thank and repay her for all her devotion and self-sacrifice. *His* success would be *her* success.

Who hasn't dreamed of a mom like Janet? She was the class mother who made the cupcakes with M&M toppings for the school picnic, the mom who sewed the greatest Halloween costume so you would win first prize, the mom who stayed up nights and did your science project so you'd get the A you truly "deserved," the mom who got mindless part-time jobs just so she could buy you whatever you wanted, no matter the cost, and no matter what your father said. She was Super-Mom, the woman who had all the time in the world just for you. Forget Daddy, forget your grandparents, and forget anyone else—*you* were the only one who mattered!

As my cousin said about *Mildred Pierce*, "Wow! What a great mom!"

But great for whom? Certainly not for Janet, and not really for her son.

Mommy's Little Monster

"You're my little angel," she'd croon to him. "When you are a big, grown-up boy, you'll make Mommy very happy. *You'll* be my happiness and you'll be successful because of me. We'll share the success."

What Janet failed to see was that this relationship was unhealthy for both her and her son. She was smothering him with "love," and there inevitably came a time when he couldn't wait to get away from her. Janet felt that her child would be forever grateful to his doting parent for everything she had done for him. And why not? If the parent was always there for the child, always making sure the child succeeded, surrounding him with her presence, giving her all, then that child would surely reward the parent.

When her son was in elementary school, he began to avoid his mother. He hated that she came to every game, concert, and activity. It wasn't because she was the only one; other moms came, too. It was the fact that she embarrassed him in unbelievable ways. She bragged about him to anyone and everyone in earshot, and had no problem accosting his coaches or teachers if she thought her son wasn't getting every opportunity to show his abilities; in short, she was a smother-mother who made the legendary showbiz mom look like the sweetheart mom from *The Brady Bunch!*

His classmates made fun of him because she was always around. He couldn't even go to sports practice without her constant presence. Very soon he stopped telling his mother what was going on in his school. He couldn't keep her from coming to games or concerts that were common knowledge for all parents, but he didn't have to let her know about the in-class debates or the student body awards assemblies. At the age of eleven he was cautiously but deliberately making his "break."

Her single-minded devotion to her child ruined other relationships for Janet. Her parents saw their grandson becoming an angry introverted child with a suffocating mother. But she refused to listen to them and limited her son's and her own relationship with them. Friends were secondary because she needed to be available for her child. Janet didn't understand mothers who had careers and left their children with caretakers. What were they thinking? Taking care of a child was a full-time rewarding career!

Her marriage fell apart because she lived only through her son. Her relationship with her husband was nonexistent. Janet absolutely refused to leave her son with relatives to go on vacation with her husband, even for a few days. They shared nothing, and she resented it when he told her she was "overprotective and possessive."

Seeing her son's bright future, she could see her own future happiness waiting just out of sight.

Separation Priority

Janet planned her son's college career and eventual rise to fame. She would be the mother of a successful man. Life looked good. With all this "devotion" heaped on the son, some might think that a bit of it would be returned to the mother. So did Janet. However, all the years spent making sure her son knew she was the only reason he was or ever would be anything good completely backfired. He rebelled.

Happiness isn't...

... living through the accomplishments of others. You owe it to yourself to pursue your own dreams and to take pleasure and satisfaction in your own accomplishments. Invest in you.

His first open act of defiance came when he was ready to go to college. He refused to go to the one his mother wanted for him. Instead he chose a university near where his father lived, miles away from her. He wanted to get away from what he saw as an emotional vampire of a woman. She was draining the life out of him! His exhaustion turned into resentment, and that soon turned into anger. He wanted and needed his own life with his own friends and he didn't want to have to "share" either his success or his personal life with his mother. Her longed-for joy never came.

Janet's ex-husband tried to explain that their son needed to distance himself from her for a while. Though he disagreed with her excessive mothering, he was gentle in his talks with her because he knew how hurt she was.

"He needs to fly a little on his own, Janet. He'll never

learn how if you hover over him. Let him be. He'll come around after a bit."

But the truth had more of a sting in it than even his father knew. Janet's son wanted nothing more than to escape a woman who constantly reminded him that he would have been nothing without her. The fact that she had created no relationships and done nothing for herself made her a fool in his eyes. Quite frankly, he was tired of her constant clinginess and her lack of a life outside of his.

He was exhausted hearing her talk about how her life and his were intertwined. And that idiotic constantly repeated statement that his success was her success filled him with anger. He felt that anything he accomplished wasn't due to her efforts; it was due to his own hard work and intelligence. Any success he might have was not hers, it was his and his alone. Didn't she realize that?

Janet felt that her son had turned against her, but what she failed to see was that he was only doing what was normal for a grown child. He was having a life of his own. She couldn't understand why he wasn't grateful for everything she had done.

"He doesn't appreciate anything I did. It was all for him. What better gift could I have given him than *always* being there for him?"

Actually, the best gift that Janet *could* have given her son would have been to live a full life herself, a life that had its own success story. This would have taken nothing away from him. It would simply have shown him how to live a complete life, one that contained more than just a suffocating mother–child relationship.

Motherhood should never be a case of "self-identity" theft. You need to make the right choices that will ensure a normal and respectful relationship between you and your children. Learn how to enhance your children's lives without neglecting your own.

YOUR LIFE, THEIR LIVES: KEYS TO SUCCESSFULLY COMBINING PARENTHOOD WITH A PERSONAL LIFE

Life needs balance.

In the same way you need a balanced diet to be physically healthy, you need balance in your life to remain emotionally healthy. Being totally committed to any one thing or person is draining. Your life should be made up of different sections. Understand that family and relationships, though very important, are just one part of your life. Life changes, children grow up, people come and go. *You* are the one constant in your world.

Respect your own talents and gifts.

Reserve an area of your life that is just for your personal growth as a person. Whether that includes a career choice, a career change, or a passionate hobby is up to you. Growth as an individual is a necessary ingredient in being a whole person. Care for yourself and respect what is important to you. This is not a selfish act. There is great value in respecting yourself and seeing your life as important.

Don't bask in reflected glory; be your own brilliant sun.
Wanting your happiness to come through your children
and their achievements *is* selfish and a waste of your own
talents and gifts. Applaud what your family members
achieve but don't forget to be just as appreciative when
you excel at something. Don't diminish what *you* can do.

Teach your children that you matter.
Children learn much from their parents. Having them see
you as a person other than Mom is good for them. Allow
them to see you as a talented, interesting person with a
life separate from theirs. With this type of role model, your
children will become adults with a strong sense of self.

You have a responsibility to yourself as well as your child.
If you do decide to become a parent, you do have a responsibility to provide your child with a healthy, safe, loving,
and protected life. But that parental responsibility does not
mean that you cease to exist as a person. You owe it to yourself to plan for the day when your children are on their own.
The empty-nest syndrome felt by past generations needn't
be the traumatic experience it once was thought to be.

Women in their forties, fifties, and older are still vital
and productive when their children leave the nest. The
new chapter of their lives should be exciting and fulfilling.
A whole new world awaits.

MOTHERHOOD MAKE-OVER 101: LESSONS LEARNED

A little quiz for you on how you view your own importance
in your life is a good way to determine your self-worth.

Do you have "good" things kept in a closet that you'll
    use someday?
Are the good china and crystal used only for company
    or to pass on to your children?
What does that tell you about how you treat yourself?

Using the good china is an analogy for your life. By not
using your very best items for yourself, you're saying that
you're not worthy of the best. In essence, you are diminish-
ing your life by not having the pleasure of the very beautiful things you would not hesitate to offer to others. Why do
you treat yourself so shallowly?

A friend had what she called a secret vice. She bought
the softest, most expensive French silk sheets she could
find. She had a linen closet full of these sheets in a beautiful variety of pastel colors. Her sister-in-law once accused
her of being extravagant and asked her why she *needed*
the silk sheets when cotton was what other people had.

My friend replied that she didn't *need* them, she
wanted them.

"If I don't indulge myself in this manner, then I'm saying that my life isn't worth sleeping on silk sheets. The
sheets are a metaphor for self-worth and a celebration of
me. My life is deserving of silk sheets. It is nourishment
for my inner me."

Remember this nourishing thought. Don't treat your
life as second best.

Celebrate you and use the good china.

Invite yourself to the feast of life. Be a participant,
not an observer. Don't watch others enjoy all your labors
and then make yourself be pleased and happy to eat the

leftover crumbs from their plates. Even if they were to be "crumbs from Caesar's table," they're still crumbs. You will never be satisfied with them. You will *always* starve.

It is the same with mothering. If you think of yourself last, you risk having only bits and leftovers from another's life. You are saying that you are not worthy of being invited to the "feast." You starve yourself emotionally.

Happiness is like food. The crumbs from *another's* happiness are just that: crumbs. They will never fill you with your own happiness.

Reclaim Your Identity

You had a life before you became a mother; you need to refer to yourself, and more importantly see yourself, as more than someone's mom. Living your own life is the best gift you can give to others.

Does that advice sound strange? It isn't. Being the sacrificial lamb in the hope that others will love, appreciate, and be eternally grateful to you doesn't work. They won't. If you dedicate your life to providing for the wants of others, you will do yourself a great disservice. You will never have this minute, this hour, this day, this week, this month, this year of your life again. You deserve to have a fulfilling life, too.

Never live through the achievements of others. Have your own dreams and your own chances for success. Be your own example of actually *living* well. Explore your own talents. Become an accomplished person others can admire. The truth is that by taking care of yourself and doing what gives you pleasure, you lead a more satisfying life. You then have more to give to another person.

Don't just let your life slip by while you talk about and praise other people's accomplishments. Be the one *others* talk about and praise!

CHAPTER 4

⚷ The Key to Becoming Your Own Person
Being a Good Little Girl No Matter Your Age

"Good little girls" become women who are the backbone of every family. They are the good daughters and sisters who are the peacemakers, the ones who do what is right for everyone but themselves. Responsible, good little girls.

In the early 1950s sociologists recorded a family situation that was a holdover from Old World societies. In many families there was always one sister who was designated by her siblings as the one who would live at home and take care of the parents. It was expected of her and considered to be her duty. These women were also the same sisters who were sometimes referred to as "little mothers" by their parents because they were expected to help care for, if not actually raise, their siblings. Some had jobs outside the home, but these were usually mundane positions taken to augment the household income. None of them had careers or any social life outside of family gatherings or attending religious services.

These women gave up a great part of their personal lives to play the part of the dutiful daughter and became the breadwinner, housekeeper, errand runner, and eventually nurse for their parents. The fact that the stay-at-home dutiful child was, with rare exceptions, a daughter is a sobering note.

Fast-forward sixty years and the role of caretaker is one still predominantly held by women. Though daughters today have relationships and marriages and homes of their own, they still strive to be the good little girl. Whether in their thirties, forties, fifties, or even sixties, women seem to be the ones who are responsible for their aging parents.

ESTELLE'S STORY

Estelle grew up in a family of three siblings. She had an older sister and a younger brother. Even though she was the youngest daughter, certain responsibilities seemed to fall on her. While her older sister enjoyed an active social life, complete with many extracurricular activities after school, Estelle was required to pick up her brother, the "baby," after school, give him his snack, and make dinner if her mother was still at work. Her brother, four years younger than she, had no responsibilities. He was the son, after all.

Her mother liked to joke that Estelle was like a "little old lady," so serious was she in everything she was asked to do. She was a responsible child.

"You're a good little girl, Estelle," her parents always told her.

When Estelle was a senior in high school, her sister, who was twenty-two, decided to get married. The wedding she had planned was a blowout celebration that would cost a tremendous amount of money, something for which her parents weren't prepared.

Estelle had plans to attend an Ivy League university, and her parents had set aside a nice amount for her tuition. Her sister complained that it wasn't fair that Estelle was getting a free ride to college when she herself had gone straight to work after high school. Then she played the guilt card: Since her parents hadn't had to pay for her tuition, she felt they owed her a big wedding in its place. She made a mini crisis out of it all.

Her parents were conflicted, and to keep peace in the family Estelle gave in to her sister's demands. Though her parents had said they would apply for a loan for Estelle's tuition, she said no. Even though she personally felt her sister had been selfish in demanding an expensive wedding, she didn't feel like she should burden her parents with more debt for college. She reasoned that they were getting older and didn't need to be paying off a large loan for years to come.

Responsible girl that she was, Estelle wanted to make sure everyone else was taken care of and happy first. Hadn't she been doing that since she was a child? She settled for a local college and got a part-time job to help out with expenses at home. Her mother told her she was a good sister for understanding.

Estelle dated sporadically, only because between school and work there really was little time for anything serious. Her dates were usually a movie and then pizza and beer in her family's kitchen. No one minded going back to her parents' house after the movie; they were college students, and cash was tight.

After college, Estelle got a job as an accountant in a prestigious firm, a bus ride away into the city. The money was good and she planned to get her own apartment as soon as she could. She wanted to live in the city where life was much more exciting than in her small town. Estelle was ready to start her life. It was time.

But her brother had his sights set on a university clear across the country, and his parents were determined that he go there. Estelle had some misgivings; she had thought her brother would go to the same local college she had and live at home. She was in the process of moving out and, with her sister married and out of the house and her brother away at college, their parents would be all alone. This was another "crisis."

When she worriedly mentioned this to her brother, he came up with a solution. If Estelle would agree to live at home for four more years, he would come back home after graduating. He would enroll in grad school at her old alma mater and live at home for a while. With someone always at home, their parents wouldn't suffer from an empty nest.

Reluctantly Estelle agreed.

"You're a great sister to me. I'll never forget this. Four years will go like that," he said, snapping his fingers.

So Estelle took a loss on the security deposit she had put down for an apartment, unpacked her things, and rode the bus into the city every morning to work. Her parents were glad she was still at home, and they began to depend on her. After all she was their "good girl."

She dated a little but it wasn't anything like dating when she was in college. Men felt uncomfortable coming back to her parents' home after a night out, and the one time she went to a date's apartment, not coming home until early morning, her parents were frantic with worry. The relationships never went anywhere.

One by one Estelle's friends from high school and college began their own lives. Some began careers in other towns, cities, or even left the state for good positions. Others bought houses, married, and had families of their own. No one, except Estelle, stayed in their parents' home as adults.

A friend of Estelle's since childhood, a man who had come to see her before leaving for a job out of state, told her that she was stagnating.

"You had dreams, Estelle. You always told me that you wanted big-city lights, remember? What happened?" Estelle smiled at that memory and shook her head, but her friend continued. "Your parents don't really need you to live with them. If you're worried about them, you can always call them. Call every day if you want to, and you and your sister can take turns stopping by. Get your brother to call, too. You're not an only child, you know, Estelle. Your parents have three children and all of you should share the responsibility."

But Estelle stayed the good daughter and good sister she had always been and said nothing to her sister or brother. She didn't want to upset them.

As her brother said, four years did go like that—but in those four years there were changes that no one could foresee. Estelle's father retired, forced to take a buyout from a company that was downsizing. Her mother's job was cut to part-time status. Finances became an issue, and Estelle's salary helped out a great deal. Without her income, her parents would not be able to stay in the home they'd shared for more than forty years.

Her aunt echoed what Estelle had heard all her life: "You're a good girl, Estelle. Your parents really need you. And look at all you've done for your brother and sister!"

It's a Wonderful Life? No, It's a Sad One

Estelle's brother came back as he'd said, but he came back with an announcement. He and a friend he'd met in college were going to share a town house. They were going to start a computer business and needed their own space.

When his sister reminded him that he'd promised to move back in to keep an eye on their parents so that she could get her own place, he told her he'd made that promise at the age of eighteen. He hadn't known what he wanted to do then. As for her moving out, her brother laid a guilt trip on that.

"It's your life, 'Stel. I *guess* Mom and Dad will be okay. But don't you feel a little like you're abandoning them? Isn't this your responsibility?"

Estelle couldn't shake the good little girl persona she'd created. Her brother was right. How could she just leave her parents? Her married sister, still the social butterfly and the mother of two sons, told Estelle bluntly that she was acting selfishly for wanting to move out. Since Estelle wasn't married and didn't have to look after children, their parents were *her* responsibility. If Estelle moved out, their parents would have to find a smaller place away from everyone they knew. They couldn't keep up a big house or the financial responsibilities that went with it by themselves.

Then she threw in a zinger:

"Why do you want to live on your own at this late stage? It's not like you're a young twenty-something." Estelle was thirty-two.

So she stayed home, and rode that damn bus every morning into the city, and tried not to remember the plans she'd had.

Estelle is a sad woman who is an accountant at a prestigious firm. Attractive and in her late forties, she has never lived on her own, never gotten married, let alone had a serious relationship, because she has spent her life putting others first. She lives at home in the same room she had as a teenager, and does everything for her parents from shopping to paying bills. Her role has become a combination of daughter, companion, and now caregiver all rolled into one.

She has put any ideas for a life of her own on the back burner but still dreams that, at some point, she will be able to live her life and move to the city. Her dreams are tinged with guilt, however, because in order for her to live her *own* dreams, her parents have to *cease* to exist.

And *good* little girls shouldn't *ever* think like that.

•••

Being the good little girl doesn't necessarily require you to take care of everyone but yourself. It might also mean that you settle for less than what you really want in life by following the decisions made for you by others.

What's the difference between "settling on" and "settling for"? When you *settle on* something, you are making a well-thought-out decision; when you *settle for* something, you have made the decision to allow yourself to take second best. That was the situation for Anjali.

She settled for everything her parents gave her and in turn got nothing that she wanted.

ANJALI'S STORY

Anjali was as different culturally from Estelle as anyone could be. She came from an Indian family that had relocated to the United States years before she was born. But though they kept the traditions and the customs of their country to a certain extent, they believed they were very modern and sophisticated people. Her parents doted on her and gave her the best that money could buy. Both parents worked hard to give their little girl all the advantages they believed she should have. What did they want in return? They asked only that she be "a good and well-behaved daughter," fulfill her duty to her parents, and remember that the future brought good things to good girls. All she had to do was wait.

Anjali became resigned to the fact that her parents would make all the major decisions for her. Everything they requested of her she did. She began *waiting* for that something good that was sure to come to her. Being a well-behaved daughter, she went to the prep school her parents chose, wore the clothes they bought, and learned to play the piano when she really wanted to learn to play the guitar. Her father had said the piano was more ladylike. To please her parents Anjali learned to settle for less than what she herself wanted in life. Whenever Anjali heard her mother's friends tell her parents what a "well-behaved daughter" they had, she smiled and secretly couldn't wait for a future when she would be freed from being so well behaved *all* the time.

Decisions, Decisions! But None of Them Your Own

All decisions were made for Anjali without anyone asking her what she wanted. When she felt constricted by the decisions they made for her, whenever she wanted to do things differently or voiced her own opinion, her parents always had an answer as to why she shouldn't.

"When decisions are made, you have to live with the consequences. What if you make a wrong decision? Look at your aunt Maya! That's why we watch out for you. We know what is best. Be a good daughter. You have a duty to us."

Maya was her father's sister, a world traveler with a great job who had never married, had lots of relationships, and made all her own decisions.

Her mother and father always told her that Maya was an embarrassment to the family because she wasn't a dutiful daughter, she was a rebel. Anjali wished she could be just like her.

Some rebelliousness was bound to occur, and a major problem arose when Anjali was eighteen and wanted to buy a car. She knew exactly what kind of car she wanted, had saved money from birthdays and holidays, and had pictured herself in the driver's seat for a long time. Her parents disagreed when they saw what she'd chosen.

They told her they would find a car for her and pay for it themselves. They were older and wiser and would choose a good solid one for her, not this frivolous sporty car she had chosen. Of course the car they got for her was nothing she had ever wanted for herself; it was practical and boring. She settled for a car she was never happy driving.

When it came time for her to go to a university, her parents were the ones to choose where she should go and what she would major in as an undergraduate. They were paying for it, and that was their way of making sure she was "well behaved." Though she was unhappy about it, Anjali said nothing, but quietly took a few electives in what really interested her.

Her parents were not possessive or overbearing. They felt that their daughter would follow the same path as her mother, her aunts, and her grandmothers. Good little daughters who became good women and were rewarded by society with good reputations as learned, well-mannered married adults. Anjali would follow this same long line of obedient girls and make her parents proud.

But she had a goal that would have surprised her parents if they had known. When she was older, she would be a person on her own terms, make her own decisions, and live with the consequences, right or wrong. Just like Aunt Maya.

All through her life Anjali acquiesced to her parents' "suggestions" even when she didn't think they were the right ones for her. She wanted things to be different when she became an adult.

When she began going on job interviews, she felt that she would now be able to make her own decisions, whether they were right or wrong. Her parents of course disagreed.

"You have a duty to be near us in case we need you."

They found her a job in a company owned by a family friend. Even though she wasn't working in a place she really wanted to be, it was good enough. Again, Anjali settled for less than what she wanted. She waited for a future time to make her move.

Always Being Obedient Means Being Content with Less

When Anjali was twenty-six, her parents began questioning her about getting married. In the tradition of their culture, they were anxious that their daughter be comfortable and complete—and that meant married with a husband and children. They carefully scrutinized each man she dated to see if he was a prospective son-in-law. Their daughter smiled at their questions because she didn't want to get married anytime soon, maybe never. Anjali wanted a career. She wanted to be a woman who was financially able to take care of her own needs, travel at will, go out with friends, and answer to no one but herself.

Her parents had other ideas for their well-behaved daughter. They kept up the pressure about marriage and finally said that if Anjali couldn't or wouldn't start to seriously look for a husband herself, they would find one for her. She thought they were just kidding. After all, arranged marriages were certainly something out of old fairy tales and antiquated traditions. Her parents were fairly modern.

Arranged marriages are quite common for women of certain cultures. The marriage contract is treated the same as a business partnership. Although divorce is never mentioned, the duties of husband and wife are stipulated much as in a prenuptial agreement. No surprises, no shocks, everything is spelled out before the ceremony. Many arranged marriages are as successful as any other.

Anjali soon found out that her parents were not kidding in the least about an arranged marriage. They were dead serious, and they were delighted when they were able to tell her they had found someone for her. His family was more than willing to meet her, and the young man seemed anxious as well. They told her that this marriage would be good for her and for *them*.

"We're getting older. We need you close to us. Be good about this, Anju."

The planned meeting was to be a dinner at their home next Saturday. Anjali dismissed what her parents told her and said that she couldn't come home that weekend. She had too much to do at work. And she was not interested in an arranged marriage. That was certainly not what modern women did.

Now the pressure began, with not only her parents calling her but her aunts, uncles, and cousins as well. The family rallied around her parents. Anjali felt overwhelmed.

"Just see him, Anju," said a recently married cousin. "You might like him and if you don't, well, there are others your parents know."

Anjali was surprised at her cousin's comment and said, "*You* think it's okay to have an arranged marriage? You got to *choose* a husband for yourself. *My* choice now is to be single for a long time. Shouldn't I be the one to make a decision that will seriously affect my life?"

But her cousin reminded Anjali that she wasn't getting any younger and that most men were looking for a young wife. She also told her that she should be a respectful daughter—which was another way of saying obedient.

"You should be thankful that your parents care enough to find you a husband. Don't you feel guilty not listening to them? Do you want to end up like our aunt Maya?"

Why not? thought Anjali. At least she's independent. She greatly admired this rebel aunt she had only seen at a few family gatherings, but she said nothing.

With so much pressure from family, and surprisingly even from some of her closest friends, Anjali agreed to meet the man her parents had chosen. There were no sparks, there was no connection between them.

Anjali dated him out of a sense of duty to her parents. There really was nothing wrong with him except that he wasn't the type of man she liked.

But after a year of what her parents called serious dating, they pressured Anjali to get engaged. Even though she wasn't happy with the suggestion, she did it to please her parents. It was only an engagement, maybe she would be able to break it off at some point.

Within another year, however, she was a married woman. Her aunt Maya, looking happy, pretty, and with a handsome man by her side, came to the wedding and gave a large money gift. When Maya asked Anjali if she was in love with her new husband, Anjali answered rather defensively that her bridegroom was a good man. Her aunt smiled sadly and replied, "He may be *a good* man, Anjali, but is he good *for you?*"

Anjali wasn't in love with him and never would be. Holding his hand was like holding that of a cousin or brother, and there was no passion in his kisses. In fact, while having sex Anjali made up lists of things in her head she had to do the next day. And she thought a lot about what her aunt had said. It wasn't "I'm glad he's good to you," but "Is he good *for you?*" That was a strange thing to say.

He was, as she told her friends, not what she had wanted . . . but he was good enough. The only thing that kept Anjali sane was her career. She loved being an insurance analyst. At work, she felt alive and in charge analyzing and solving problems alone in her small cubicle.

A few years later her parents began hinting at grandchildren; they wanted to become grandparents before it was too late. Anjali's husband was agreeable to becoming a father. All three felt that a child would cement the marriage. Anjali wasn't sure, and she refused to be convinced to have a child when she didn't want one. She even refused to talk about it. Her parents could not persuade their well-behaved daughter to become a mother.

Anjali tried to explain that she wanted a life separate from just being a wife. She felt that once she had a child, her career would be over and she would be only someone's wife and someone's mother. Besides, she didn't think it was fair to bring a child into a marriage where the mother wasn't in love with the father.

Her marriage became strained because her husband believed that one of a couple's responsibilities in life was to have children. She soon found that she and her husband were now living in the same house with less in common than before. They lived like this for several more years, attending family gatherings and events only going through the motions of being a married couple. People, her mother said, were talking.

"Be a good daughter, Anjali. Good things come to good girls," she said. However, *girl* was the wrong word for her mother to use. Hearing it said in reference to a woman in her thirties made Anjali understand for the first time exactly how she was seen by her parents, her family, and maybe even her husband. Girls were obedient and Anjali was no longer a girl, good or bad. She was a woman, and she was entitled to make her own decisions.

She became angry first at her parents and then at herself for living a life she didn't want. She knew now what her aunt had meant about someone being good *for you.* Anjali hated living like this and finally told her husband she wanted a divorce. She was not one of the women who were comfortable in an arranged marriage.

Happiness isn't...

... always being the good little girl for everyone else.

Make *your* life priority number one. Remember that by always being the responsible one, the peacemaker, the good little girl, you are making life good for everyone ... but you.

Anjali was tired of being miserable, tired of being married to a good man, and tired of living a life she hated. And she was more than tired of settling for what she didn't want and waiting for something good to happen simply because she was "obedient."

Obedient good girls seemed to only reap what other people saw as rewards: a home, marriage, and children. None of these were terrible things, but they were not what she wanted for herself. Like her storied aunt Maya of family legend, Anjali had to rebel against what everyone else wanted *for her* to get what *she* wanted. What she wanted was freedom to be herself. That would be her reward.

Her family was tremendously upset and tried to dissuade her from "a bad decision," but Anjali was finally going to do what she wanted to do. She had made the decision that she would never again settle for anything she didn't want. A divorce was what she wanted and what she was getting. When they ominously mentioned that she would end up like the family black sheep, Maya, Anjali responded, "At least she gets to make her own decisions!"

A year after she and her husband had their marriage legally dissolved, Anjali called me to talk about life after divorce. It was, she said, very freeing. She was learning to be self-reliant, make her own decisions, and deal with any consequences her decisions might bring. She finally "owned" her life.

"You know, I was never my own person. I was my parents' daughter, I was my husband's wife. I never belonged to *me.*"

Anjali went on to say that it had been a year of great changes for her, some good, some not so good, but a year in which she learned to start to become the woman she wanted to be. And by learning that, Anjali is being a good girl who obeys her own wishes and makes sure she gets what she wants in the present and in the future.

WHOSE LIFE IS IT? SURPRISE, IT REALLY IS YOURS!

We all have an image of who we want to be. Sometimes that image can conflict dramatically with who we really are. Planning your life so that it helps to achieve your dreams is healthy and normal. While no one would fault you for having your parents' best interests at heart, those interests should not keep you from living a full life. There is also nothing wrong with knowing that while your parents want only what is best for you, as an adult you may differ with them about what really *is* best for your life.

Estelle was the good little girl, but she allowed her siblings and her parents to disregard what mattered to her. In their lives, her plans came in third place—if they were even considered at all. The hard fact is, she encouraged this dismissive behavior by being "good and responsible" at all times.

In the case of Anjali, she had tradition and culture with which to contend as well as her parents' ideas and pressure about family ties. Her obedient behavior reflected well on her parents. When she abided by their decisions, it was seen as honoring them.

However, regardless of the individual situation, you have to let your family know that you have plans and a design for your own life.

State Your Own Terms: The Keys to Create the Blueprint for Your Life

Take yourself out of the picture.
Define the expressions *good* and *responsible* as they relate to your parents and siblings. Do you understand them as meaning that you have to sacrifice your own life for them? You shouldn't, and neither should they. Always being obedient is learning to be content with less.

Visualize what would happen if you were not always available for every small crisis or made your own decisions. What would happen if you weren't always nearby?

Would the world really end? No. You will be surprised at how everyone and everything will and can adjust without your help or obedient agreement. Don't allow anyone to tell you that you are the sole person who can make their world run smoothly.

Deal with guilt.

Guilt is an exclusive human emotion, and we all have felt it at some point. Ask yourself this question, though: Exactly what are you guilty of doing? Certainly wanting to have a life outside of your parents is nothing to feel guilty over. Think about how you can accommodate both your filial obligations and your own personal and career goals. Understand that you cannot view your life or time as a throwaway. *You* should be your primary concern. The pursuit of your own dreams isn't a selfish way to live. You give in to *someone else's* selfish demands, no matter how politely requested, when you don't live the way you want to live.

Speak up.

Don't grit your teeth and give in to others if it means you are going to lose out. Had Estelle told her parents that no way was she giving up a priceless education at an Ivy League school just so her tuition money could be blown in one night on a big wedding reception for her sister, they more than likely would have listened. And she should have said the same to her sister. Being the peacemaker cost her a lot.

By always allowing her parents to make decisions on her behalf even when she became an adult, Anjali put herself in the backseat. Had she told them she was going to make her own choices about what she knew was best for her as a woman, and had she firmly stuck to her stance, her parents may have protested, but they would have had to let go.

Don't readily agree to what others ask of you.

Write your life in the middle of the page . . . *not in the margins.*

Think of yourself as the architect of your own life, and then think about what architects do—they put their ideas and designs on the *entire* page. No architect would think of only using the margins for her plans, and neither should you. You are not an appendage of your parents, you are a separate individual with a mind and a life to live.

By always being agreeable, you are inviting others to take advantage of you. You need to disagree for your own benefit. Though they may not admit it, others will respect you more for actually standing up for your rights.

Don't see your life as an afterthought.

If you had the choice of whether to fly first class or coach, you know exactly what you would choose. Live your life on your own terms and don't make it second class. It isn't wrong to think of yourself first, it is practical. You are the only one who can give yourself a first-class ticket. Even the person who wishes nothing but the absolute best for your life cannot buy you that ticket. Do not live your life only when it is convenient for others.

Be irresponsible sometimes.
Come on now! Being the "responsible" one all the time is a draining and unsatisfying way to live, and it isn't much fun. Refuse to take *all the responsibility* all the time. Be a bit misbehaved. Expect and demand fairness; your life is not disposable. It is a gift, so treat it as one. The main key to becoming your own woman is learning to become selfish in a good way.

Decide exactly what you want to do with your life. Ask yourself these questions:

Who do you want to be?
What makes you feel fulfilled?
How do you want to live?
Where do you want to live?

The choices should be yours.

BECOMING YOU: A PURPOSE OF VISION

Simply defined, purpose of vision is what you want and how you want to live. Doing something just because others have done so *before* you or because you have been told that that is what you *should* do is not in your best self-interest.

On my desk there is a framed saying that I cherish. It reads: *You are not what you were born, but what you have it in yourself to become.*

That saying should reflect the way you live your life. If you follow what "well-meaning" people tell you to do, you will be miserable. You will be buried in an unhappy life and never become the "you" you have it inside yourself to be. Make decisions that will benefit you.

Who do you want to be? In the case of a man named Archibald Leach born in abject poverty, the answer was that he wanted a much better life, a life of abundance and happiness. Archie found it when he became the sophisticated actor Cary Grant. He had a purpose of vision.

WHAT "GOOD LITTLE GIRLS" SHOULD DO 101: LESSONS LEARNED

Have you ever found a lock so rusted that even its key can't open it? Years of certain unchanging conditions have literally glued it shut. Your mind-set can be as rusty as that lock if you've kept it shut for any length of time. Besides the key, you need to help yourself smooth the way and scrape away a rusty way of thinking that no longer serves you well.

It helps to remember that no one *gives* you the power over your own life. By taking control of your own life, you empower yourself. Habitual negative thinking becomes the rust that covers your mind. Either it is the way you have been taught to think about responsibility, or you've somehow adopted antiquated ideas about how you *should* think.

No matter how you learned these thought processes, it is a form of thinking that stops you from finding your own joy.

The good little girl is another myth that makes women feel they must put the happiness of others before their own. It is never wrong to think of yourself first and to decide what is right for you. You deserve a life. Always being the good little girl is good for everyone else *but* you!

CHAPTER 5

The Key to Love and Self-Acceptance
I Don't Deserve to Be Happy Until the Thin Lady Sings

KRISTEN'S STORY

It is a simple fact learned in any introduction to psychology class: When you *think* you look good, you *feel* good. Everything in life seems a bit better because you feel good about your looks. Feeling satisfied with your appearance makes a tremendous amount of difference in how you present yourself to the world. Some women live their entire lives on their perception of their physical selves.

How do you feel about body image and, more important, how do you relate it to your own life? For some women, the way they think they look influences their daily lives adversely. It impacts everything they do. The most common issue women have with body image is their weight. Every day happiness hinges on what the scale in their bathrooms tells them. I was one of them.

One fateful day, on a beautiful vacation in the Bahamas where I should have been enjoying myself, but of course wasn't due to my unattainable "conditions" for happiness, a remark from my husband, a comment about how I never *allowed* myself to be happy, struck a chord deep inside me. We were having dinner in a five-star restaurant when I pulled out my crumpled calorie counter. The scale in the bathroom (how *dare* resorts have a scale in the bathroom!) had not given me the right number, and so I was counting calories again.

My husband looked at me, smiled sympathetically, shook his head, and said, "Don't you ever *allow* yourself to enjoy *anything?* You're sabotaging any chance you have to enjoy this beautiful vacation."

The fact that he made the remark at all not only surprised me but annoyed the hell out of me! *Me?* Not *allow* myself to be *happy?* What a ridiculous thing to say! I couldn't let it go. I debated the truth of his statement. He had to be wrong about that remark! He had to be!

But . . . he was right on target. I found that as far as being happy, I was like Goldilocks in the house of the Three Bears: I wanted everything to be "just right." And it wasn't simply weight; it was every aspect of my life. I felt I wasn't deserving of happiness. I had to weigh a certain "just right" weight, my work had to be perfect, my relationships needed to be not just good but great. As incredible as it sounds, even the weather had to be "just right" before I felt I deserved to be happy. I was a master at sabotaging my chances for happiness.

Body image is unique to our modern culture. We are flooded with images from the media of what we *should* look like. Any deviation from this ideal makes us a "bad" person, someone who has done something wrong in not attaining perfection. While the sane, conscious part of your mind tells you that there is something deeply wrong with this ideal image, the subconscious, impressionable you says differently. You want to have the beautiful image, you need to be thought of as deserving. You long to be the "thin lady."

My best friend looks at the pictures of the Caribbean vacation my husband and I took last year. There we are, aboard a blue sailboat, smiling as we pose for a picture with the resort's sailing master.

"I like your swimsuit," says my friend. "That's a really nice color for you. You two look great."

"Thanks," I sigh, and then tell her how much I weighed when the picture was taken.

If I show you pictures of all the places I have been in my life, I can give you minute details about the place itself, the food, the sights, and the weather. I can also tell you something else simply by looking at those pictures: the exact number on the scale I was at that particular time in my life.

It's been this way with any pictures taken of me from my teen years on; no matter where I was, no matter what I was doing, I can remember the number on the scale at that exact time. For me, almost everything related to weight and trying to be the perfect number. Even though I knew I looked good, was once a professional dancer, still danced for exercise, and played a wicked game of tennis, the fact was that I wasn't the perfect number society said someone of my build should be. I was always just a little off the mark. It bothered me that I had trouble reaching and maintaining that number. According to my convoluted way of thinking, I didn't *deserve* happiness. I couldn't allow myself to be satisfied with me! I'd never get to where I wanted to be if I was happy with myself!

Rather than seeing myself as the sum of many good parts, I saw only one thing: my failure to achieve the perfect number. I was obsessed with being *the* number, and I allowed that number on the scale to dictate all the events in my life. The number even dictated the clothes I wore. My editor in chief joked that the pashmina shawls I invariably wore as cover-ups when attending the annual awards ceremony were a part of my "formal night out" uniform.

Weight and sizes are the bane of modern women. We may be intelligent, we may be highly skilled in our field, we may even have received awards for our accomplishments, but the idea that we are "overweight" can negate all of it. It is similar to the feeling we get when we're beautifully dressed to go out and suddenly find a small chip in our nail polish. That little chip has a greater impact on us than our overall image. It shouldn't, but it does; we can't stop thinking about it.

Media phenomenon Oprah Winfrey and best-selling novelist Anne Rice—both immensely successful and powerful women in their respective fields—are no less concerned about extra pounds than you or I am.

Both have mentioned their "problems with weight" in interviews. These are women whom we admire and see as strong, determined females, yet when it comes to weight, they become one of the millions of women who also face the daily struggle of the pounds.

The idea of being overweight is a constant nagging feeling of despair at not being personally successful in "controlling" your own body. What good is being in control of finances, major companies, and businesses if you're not in control of your body?! Silly idea, right? And yet that is exactly the unconscious thought many intelligent women have.

Go to a meeting of any of the popular weight loss organizations and you will hear women talking about being "thin and happy." It seems they don't feel deserving of happiness because they don't fit media images of what women should look like. A few extra pounds are considered a disaster.

It isn't just weight that affects our concepts of image; it also has to do with beauty of face, body, even height. We are all dissatisfied with some part of the creature we are. Nose, eyes, breasts, legs, stomach, and buttocks come under our daily scrutiny and sometimes under the plastic surgeon's knife. The idea that we would be happy if we could change certain physical attributes is a false one. Again, we are putting a condition on when and how we are allowed to be happy. We look to find happiness by physically altering our bodies in one way or another.

How can you change your thinking about body image, still keep the parts of yourself that make you successful, make peace with the body you have now, and be happy?

I have had many conversations with friends and colleagues who had, at one time or another, made a negative statement about how bad they thought they looked, and of course there were letters and e-mails from readers on the same topic. I certainly knew a body image problem existed not only for me but for all women.

It had to do with perception. Everyone was either punishing themselves because their body type wasn't what they were led to believe it should be, or, like me, they were waiting to be happy once they had achieved the perfect weight. And that was likely to be a long, long wait.

I needed to devote a chapter in my book to helping successful intelligent women change their perception of perfect and stop denying themselves happiness.

All good writing begins with the author's research. Mine began by taking a trip into the past; the sixteenth century, to be exact.

Too Thin for Michelangelo?

I made a lunch date with a friend who is a director at a museum and whose expertise is the female form of the 1500s. Talking with him would give me a perspective on body image. After lunch we walked through the permanent exhibit of Renaissance art in the museum as he pointed out the paintings of women nude and in all stages of dress and undress. He astutely answered my questions about body image.

Happiness is . . .

. . . accepting yourself.

Be realistic in your goals. If you want to make physical changes, set small achievable goals. In other words, don't plan to have an entire body lift if you're unhappy about the bags under your eyes! It is the same with weight. Losing ten pounds instead of fifteen isn't bad. Small changes add up to bigger ones.

"If you look at these paintings, not one of the women can be called ugly or overweight, yet they are as completely different from one another as parakeets are to parrots. It is all a matter of taste and preference. The fact that has always impressed me is that every one of them seems to be very comfortable in her own body. Obviously the artists thought so, too, since they chose to celebrate the form of these women and immortalize them for all the ages. Women of today are no different, not really. Beauty is never simply one look or one size. Beauty is variety."

As I looked at the paintings, I had to admit that what he said was true.

All sizes, all shapes, some curvier than others, but all were beautiful. Some had what we refer to as love handles; some had soft, fuller stomachs that had never suffered through crunches in a gym. Though I had seen them many times before, it was actually refreshing to view them in a new light.

As I was about to leave, my friend looked at me and gave me a compliment of sorts.

"By the way, you yourself could never be a model for Michelangelo or Leonardo or really for any of the masters of that era."

How true, I thought. No way could I be a model for the masters. I sighed as he went on.

"Actually, Kristen, they would consider you too *thin*. Think about that."

And though I didn't quite believe *anyone* from *any* century would ever consider *me* "too thin," I did think about what he'd said all the way home.

Even Beautiful People Get Airbrushed

My next stop was something that I had to do for professional reasons, but it would certainly count as research. I was scheduled to have professional photos taken for my newspaper.

The photographer's studio where I was sent was famous for preparing quality portfolios for models, actors, and dancers. The waiting room was filled with perfect, gorgeous females. Being in a room with these women was like being at beauty pageant. Each one was breathtakingly beautiful; each exuded a sexy confidence. Surrounded by women whose livelihood was based in large part on their physical appearance, I didn't think I'd find anyone among them who had a negative body image.

But, as I was later to find out, I was wrong.

The photo shoot was an eye opener in many ways. Professionally dressed and with hair and makeup done by experts, and with soft lighting, I stood, sat, and smiled for an hour while the photographer coaxed and cajoled me into pose after pose.

With all the before-photo-shoot preparation, I knew I had to look more than good in person. But what about the actual pictures? Would my mind still see what I perceived as the wrong weight number? (Of course I had weighed myself that morning. Great start to wanting to change my *own* perception of body image!)

Doing a quick analysis of my images that the photographer had put up on the computer, I was pleasantly surprised that I actually liked what I saw. I didn't see a woman who looked as if she needed to lose weight; instead I saw someone who looked fit and attractive.

The photographer asked if there was anything I wanted changed in the photos, and I pointed out a few. "We can airbrush any imperfections," the photographer said as he erased a noticeable scar on my collarbone. I'd known about airbrushing but I was impressed that it was so easy. I told him that, with all the beautiful women I had seen in his studio, he probably didn't have to do much airbrushing.

"Oh, no, we do this all the time. No one is completely satisfied with their image. They all manage to find some fault with themselves, even women we would call natural beauties. Believe me, everyone wants airbrushing."

A few days after having my picture taken, I knew I needed to see if the "real" me matched up with the made-up, dressed-up me from the photo shoot. To do that, I had to enter the scariest place of all. I had to enter the Mirror Zone.

BODY IMAGE REALITY: KEYS TO A HEALTHY, REALISTIC BODY IMAGE

Love and accept.

The first key to love and acceptance of self begins with looking at yourself in a full-length mirror. That can be a scary thought, but following the advice of a friend, a plastic surgeon, I had what she terms the mirror experience. Before she will even schedule any type of surgery, she asks her patients to study themselves in a full-length mirror and find two things about their image that they particularly like. She then focuses on what her patient tells her. If someone likes her mouth or the shape of her face, she knows that this is a good candidate for surgery. If a woman hates everything about herself, my friend will refer her for counseling.

"Truly look at yourself and find what pleases you. Once you have something you like about your image, you can go on from there. If you want to make some changes, do it, but at least you know there are parts of yourself that you do find attractive."

Mirror, mirror . . . at least let me like what I see!

We look in mirrors every day, but we don't really see ourselves. We're usually too rushed to see the good parts. All we notice is what we don't like. The mirror tells no lies, hides no flaws, and is the real you. With or without flattering lighting, the image reflected back is what the world sees and what you need to love. For me, as for many women, this is difficult. It's different from looking at pictures; this image is you up close and personal, in the flesh. If you're not brave enough to face the naked truth, you at least need to be in panties and a bra.

Facing the mirror and finding a person you love is probably the most difficult part of making a much-needed change in your thinking—but it is a necessary part. If you can't find beauty in the person you see looking back at you every day, then you have a bigger problem than you know.

My mirror experience was similar to truly observing a painting. I scrutinized myself, turning this way and that, getting all angles and making myself stare at the woman I was. I closed my eyes and sighed. All I could find was fault after fault. I walked out of the room. Maybe I wasn't ready for this. But I knew I had to do it for myself. I had to *like* what I saw and I had to *love me,* as hard as that might be.

Back to the mirror, this time determined to see something I liked.

Again I turned, looked with a critical eye, and laughed at what I was doing. But . . . there was *something* about my image that made me smile. I liked my green eyes; I thought my smile was cute. I did have curves but I also had a good waistline. I had strong legs from dancing and tennis. I could work on my stomach much more to get it firmer, but all in all I did like what I saw. Okay, I thought, all right.

Looking at my image I thought, If *this* is who I am, well, it's not bad, not bad at all. I could like the woman in the mirror. The image was certainly not a cause for denying myself happiness. The nagging "wrong number" seemed to be far away from the reality I saw. Maybe that number and I will never get together—but so what? The number is just a number. It may be a little higher than I like, but it shouldn't have the power to control my happiness.

Buy what fits and throw out the scale.

A personal shopper I interviewed a few years ago for an article I was writing on fashion gave me priceless advice for buying and wearing clothes. It is the same advice she gives to her celebrity clients.

"Buy what fits, Kristen, *never, ever* focus on the size. Play a little mind game with yourself—pretend you *are* the perfect number. It may seem a little silly, but it works. Then clean out your closet. If you haven't worn an outfit in two years, get rid of it. *And* for God's sake, throw out the scale!"

Good advice and of course I had never heeded it, but now it was time I did. I stopped buying a size hoping to fit into it by a certain date. That's a defeatist attitude right there because it means I don't like me now. Looking good makes you feel good. You're not going to feel good wearing clothes that don't fit or looking at beautiful outfits hanging in your closet you can't wear because they don't fit. "Clothes-hoping-to-be worn," with store tags still on them, were given away.

The odious metallic digital monster called a scale, with its big glaring numbers, was put in the basement. Checking my weight was a sort of punishment I inflicted on myself every morning. If I wasn't satisfied with the number, it colored my entire day. How can you hope to be happy when you start off every morning with a negative image of yourself?

Buying clothes that actually fit and not making myself miserable with the scale had a great effect on my attitude. The number that fits is perfect.

You are your own vision of perfection—invest in you! If you knew there was some product that would add immeasurably to your quality of life, emotionally and physically, allow you to have peace of mind, and give you a surefire way to be happy, you would buy it in a heartbeat.

That is exactly what will happen when you invest in yourself.

Being constantly critical of your body image undermines your emotional health and creates a pattern of negativity that is hard to break. What you think about yourself affects everything about you—your relationships, your job, your entire life! You may never take a trip to the Kingdom of Magical Numbers, so stop beating yourself up over the perfect numeral!

Truthfully, we all have parts of ourselves that we would love to change. I would never tell someone not to lose weight or not to have cosmetic surgery if she truly wanted it for a good reason—not just to fit a generic "beauty" image conjured up by Madison Avenue.

If you put twenty women in a room, you would see twenty different versions of beauty. That includes everything from coloring to height to weight. There is no "one size fits all" in beauty, or anything else in life really, and that's as it should be.

Make an inventory of all your good qualities. Write them down. Look at yourself and find the person who cares enough about herself to accept who she is now. Then ask yourself if there is room for improvement. Are you willing to invest in yourself and make small changes if necessary?

Accepting you for who you are while acknowledging a need for improvement is a realistic approach to living an abundantly happy life.

Be you.

You are so worth it—but only if you believe it!

It isn't only good little slim girls who deserve to be happy (and eat chocolate). You deserve the same. Self-love is the real key, and knowing your worth unlocks the door to self-esteem.

When mega-star performer Tina Turner was showing her pricey new acquisition, a custom-made Hummer, to an interviewer, he admired it and then jokingly asked Ms. Turner if she thought she was worth it.

Ms. Turner, who'd had an impoverished childhood, had left a horribly abusive marriage, then had worked exhaustingly hard to reinvent her life and career and finally become a superstar, smiled sweetly and said, "Honey, I'm worth *much* more."

Here's a simple equation. If you know you're worth it, you are; if you don't think you're worth it, you're not. It is a mind-set. Thinking, I am so worth it gives you insight into changing your view of self-worth.

Ask yourself this question: How much *are* you worth in terms of time and money? It's a simple question, really. For many of us it is difficult to answer this question. We are led to believe our self-worth must be a reflection of our looks. So in essence, if we don't *believe* we look good, we *assume* we have no worth!

Yet self-worth should have nothing to do with looks and everything to do with an innate feeling that you really are worth it. You are worth going after dreams, you are worth being in a good relationship, you are worth living a life that fulfills and nourishes you, and you are certainly worth not having to wait to be happy "when everything is just right."

The realization is that just as you are now, you are the most important person in your life.

This is a practical reality. The real and only question you have to answer is: Do I deserve to be happy right here, right now? And the answer should be a resounding yes! Invest in your self. You are worth more than you ever believed.

Give yourself permission to be happy.

It may sound strange to say that you have to give yourself permission to be happy, but you are the only one who has the right and the power to do so. You're an adult. No one, and nothing, has the power to allow or disallow you anything. It is all up to you. Getting what you want doesn't guarantee happiness.

I interviewed a woman who'd lost more than eighty pounds on a national weight loss program. She assumed that once she lost the weight, she would feel happy. The weight was lost, she looks fabulous, but she's *still* not happy. She believed that the weight loss would change her life forever; that once she reached her goal, she'd be deserving of happiness. Unfortunately for her, that turned out not to be true. Today she's a good-looking woman with a great figure who is still unhappy.

BODY IMAGE 101: LESSONS LEARNED

One last word about body image: Physical well-being is a key to liking your body, and exercise is one way to feel good. Just as there is no generic form of beauty, there is also no one form of exercise that fits all. If you absolutely hate working out at a gym, then you will find excuses not to go. Besides, rigorous exercising is not for everyone. The days of "feel the burn" and "no pain, no gain" are, thank God, long gone.

Find something you really enjoy doing and you will be more than eager to do it. Let your exercise be fun. My best friend runs, but running is definitely not something I would enjoy. It is not for me. A co-worker power-walks, but that's not my idea of fun, either. I like dancing; that and weekend tennis keep me mentally alert and fit.

I didn't want to waste any more *time* waiting for that perfect number before I could allow myself to be happy. Happiness is a state of being, not a reward for *being* a good little girl who loses twenty pounds and has the perfect number. I will always have days when the old song of "When I lose the weight then I'll be happy" is just waiting to be played again, especially when I am under stress. But that is habit, and it was a part of my thinking for a very long time. It will take a while to break it and substitute it with a more positive song.

To be honest, I know I'll never reach the number I've been chasing all my life. I may just circle it and always be flying slightly over it—and that has to be okay. You have to make peace with yourself, and I am pretty sure I have finally done that.

While you're working on love and self-acceptance, it may be good to think of a quote by the famed sculptor Michelangelo. When an emissary of the pope asked him why he was taking *so long* to finish the ceiling of the Sistine Chapel, the great artist replied: "Questo lavoro è un lavoro in progessivo. Segue no tempo però il suo tempo."

Translation?

"This work is a work in progress. It follows no time but its own."

We are all, as the saying goes, "a work in progress." And look how well the Sistine Chapel turned out!

CHAPTER 6

The Key to Saving Yourself

The Love of a Good Woman Will Not Change a Bad Man

Women have been trying to "save" bad men from themselves since before recorded time. There were more than likely a few Cro-Magnon women who were sacrificing their own existence trying to save their Cro-Magnon males from dangerous addictions. I seriously wouldn't doubt it. It is, unfortunately, a female thing.

No one has ever satisfactorily explained why any woman goes on the save-the-bad-man campaign. Psychiatrists and sociologists certainly have their theories about why certain women try to save men from themselves, and most of it centers on some supposed emotional flaw in the women. But even the sanest, most reasonable women among us seem to have the idea that their love, patience, and support will save someone who can't or won't save himself.

This saving state of mind crosses all social strata. From the famous acting legend Katharine Hepburn trying to save the equally famous, but sadly alcoholic, Spencer Tracy, to a close friend you know who is involved in a disastrous relationship with an addict, the tale of a woman trying to save her man from himself is classic.

In *"The Love of a Good Woman . . . ,"* we meet Beth and Lauren and learn of the years, money, and wasted life opportunities each spent trying to save a man who didn't want to be saved from the addictions that were consuming his life. In the process the addictions almost consumed Beth and Lauren.

BETH'S STORY

Beth's fiancé Daniel was an addict. She knew this when they met. A weekend user, he had started his journey by taking the so-called recreational drugs on Friday and Saturday nights. He liked the mellow feeling he got from them, especially after a long week as a stock analyst. Beth thought she understood about his weekend use of drugs, and while she wasn't thrilled about it, she knew that he needed something to help him relax from all the pressure. Anyway he only used on weekends; she could deal with it for a while.

Still, sometimes she felt very uncomfortable with the effect it had on him. But she loved him and felt sure that someday soon she would help him see that he didn't really need drugs in his life. She could save him.

Daniel promised her he would stop the drugs once he was more confident in his job. He promised, but he didn't. Many promises made, many promises broken.

For three years Beth lived with seeing Daniel mellow out on weekends. He became lethargic and sometimes didn't get off the couch for two days. He was, quite literally, drugged out, and she felt like she was only there to clean up after him and make sure that he ate. She was alarmed for his health.

Strange people began calling the condo where they lived, usually very late at night. When she asked who these people were, Daniel explained it away by saying they were old friends of his whom Beth didn't know. When she pressed the issue, he became belligerent and said, "I *did* have a life *before* I met you, you know."

Beth searched the Internet for info on the dangers of recreational use of drugs and discussed Daniel's problem with her best friend. Her friend suggested that if Dan didn't seek help on his own, Beth should join a support group. Beth was sure she could help Daniel on her own so she refused to take her friend's advice. But it was hard, and about to get much harder.

Drugs, Danger, and Daniel

After a while weekend use wasn't enough; Daniel wanted the feeling all week long, and soon mellow wasn't the only way he wanted to feel. He needed to be "up," and buzz drugs became a staple in his diet, too. The late-night phone calls continued, and once Beth came home to find a sinister-looking man sitting in her living room waiting for Daniel. The stranger told her, "Danny should be right back."

Breaking out in a cold sweat, she felt an animal fear of this person. Who was he, what did he want; where the hell was Daniel? She asked him to wait outside and he bluntly refused, sitting on the couch and challenging her with his eyes to defy him.

Frightened to be alone with this man, Beth kept the door of the condo wide open, standing just inside until she heard Daniel come up the steps. He looked upset when he saw the man there and glanced at Beth nervously. But Beth, with her heart pounding, just walked to their bedroom and locked the door. She heard Daniel and the stranger talking in low agitated voices.

"You left a complete stranger in our home alone. I was terrified!" Beth angrily told him later that night. "Who is he? What does he want from you?"

Daniel tried to explain, first by saying he was someone from his old neighborhood, which Beth knew was a lie. She told him so. Then he angrily told her that she had no business questioning who his friends were. Beth stood her ground about the strange man.

"Understand this, Daniel, if anything like that happens again I'm calling the police! That man is dangerous and I swear I will have cops here in a heartbeat if I ever see him in this condo again."

Beth never saw the stranger again, and she felt it was because she had mentioned the police to Daniel. He seemed genuinely afraid of her statement.

It reminded Beth of when she had been stopped at a routine police roadblock a few months before. Daniel, who was in the passenger's seat, had seemed panicky as the policeman motioned Beth to the side of the road. He sat there with his eyes down and breathing heavily. The roadblock turned out to be for nothing more than a flooded street; police were diverting traffic. As Beth pulled away from the officer who had stopped her car, she heard Daniel exhale raggedly.

Thinking about the incident made Beth feel sure he'd had drugs in her car. If that was true, he had put them both at risk of arrest. It was a frightening way to live.

Saving Daniel

Beth had wanted to start her own business. She was an expert chef, and her dream seemed very attainable.

She had business cards made up and even began handing them out to prospective clients. There was a bright future ahead.

But Daniel's "problem" was becoming worse, and Beth felt that she had to "be there" for him. His addiction cost him his job, and she convinced him to go into rehab. Once out of rehab he swore his love for Beth and promised that he was through with drugs. His promise lasted less than a week.

Knowing she couldn't put time and energy into a new business and take care of Daniel at once, Beth took a job with a temp service that offered flexible hours.

Then began a series of episodes where Beth had to deal with Daniel's addiction in a much more unpleasant way. Money would be missing from her handbag; her name was forged on a check. She would be called to pick up a barely coherent Dan at an unknown apartment or, worse, bail him out of jail.

There were nights he didn't come home at all, and she feared the worst. The hardest time was when she received a phone call from Daniel at two o'clock in the morning begging her to come get him. Beth drove to a horrible part of the city and found Daniel alone and afraid in a dirty alley covered in his own vomit.

He promised her over and over again he would change and repeatedly tried rehab or Narc-Anon. Nothing worked for long. His vows were broken almost before they were uttered. But Beth couldn't leave Daniel. She felt guilty for not being able to help him; there must be something wrong with *her* if her love and commitment couldn't save him from himself.

Saving Beth

Despite all the hell he put Beth through, Daniel didn't really *want* to change. Beth held on, convinced that when Dan was better, she'd start her own business and they'd both be happy. She didn't want to give up on him.

After seven years of seeing her live like this, her best friend told Beth that she would always be second in Dan's life. When Beth, in surprise, asked her why she had said that, the friend replied, "Dan loves his drugs much more than he loves you."

That statement hit Beth like a brick and made her stop and think about her life with Daniel. She needed help and finally took her friend's advice. She joined a support group and for six months faithfully attended meetings.

The group meetings couldn't do anything to stop the problem, but Beth didn't feel so alone anymore; she saw there were others with the same horrible problem she was facing. However, at the meetings she also saw that there were a lot of enablers, and she knew that she was certainly one of them.

By taking care of Daniel, by bailing him out, by being a source of money for him, by spending her life with a drug addict, she was giving him the means and support to keep on being an addict. Beth hated herself for being someone who not only couldn't help Daniel get off drugs but was actually *helping* him to remain an addict.

She had never called him to account for what he was doing, not just to himself, but to her and to their life together. Beth knew she was, in reality, rewarding Daniel for his addiction and behavior. One woman in the group had been an enabler to her husband for more than twenty years. Looking at her was like looking in a mirror and seeing her older self. Beth saw what her future life with Daniel would be like, and it frightened her into action.

She wanted to be happy and saw that Daniel was preventing her from doing so. There were years of sacrifice and waste with absolutely nothing to show. It was true. He loved his drugs much more than he loved her, and Beth could no longer live that way. To be happy, she had to leave him. Saving Dan became secondary to saving Beth.

•••

Addicts and enablers are not the only ones who have a toxic relationship. There are those relationships whose partners fit both categories; each one is both an addict *and* an enabler. In those relationships, life becomes volatile and can have serious consequences that can affect you even after the relationship has ended. This is especially true when one of the partners decides to make positive changes to stop the addiction and tries to help the other do the same.

LAUREN'S STORY
Lauren met Christopher at a college where he was a political science professor. She was in her early forties, newly divorced, and finishing a degree she had long put on hold. Christopher was intelligent and passionate about politics. Lauren took his class and was flattered that he showed interest in her. She was shy about returning to school and when one night he asked her to join him after classes for drinks, she accepted.

Lauren had come out of a marriage where her husband had been unsupportive of any of her goals. He hadn't been interested in what was important to her. Married her first year in college, she had left school, always intending to go back—but the time was never right. Her husband had wanted a wife who went to work rather than to classes, and Lauren had obliged him even while she knew she was letting herself down.

Happiness is . . .
. . . giving yourself permission to be happy.
You are the only one stopping yourself from being happy. Whether it is staying in a bad relationship or trying to save a "bad" man, it is up to you to make a change in your life that will permit you to find happiness.

The fact that Christopher, a brilliant man by all accounts, encouraged her to pursue her degree was a big plus in their relationship. Living on savings and a hard-won scholarship, Lauren was determined to graduate in two years and begin a longed-for new life.

Christopher introduced Lauren to a fun intellectual crowd and to what he called "the art of drinking." She had never been much of a drinker; in fact, in her former marriage she and her husband had never even had alcohol in the house. Whenever they had entertained, she or her husband would go out to buy one bottle of whatever liquor their guests liked. Drinking just wasn't important in her life back then.

But Christopher made drinking sound sophisticated and elegant. Her education in alcohol started with wine, and she found that she liked it very much; the taste, the buzz made her feel good. Drinking became a major part of their relationship. Not being a person who drank in the past didn't stop Lauren from learning how to do it now. She soon discovered that knowing a bottle of wine or a couple of drinks were waiting for her at the end of a full day was a comforting thought.

Being with Christopher changed her mind about a lot of things. He liked having someone to share drinks with him, and he liked having late-night gatherings with his friends in his apartment where there was always a tremendous amount of alcohol. Drinking and heavy conversation was the life he lived, and Lauren was becoming a part of it. No longer a woman who was in bed by 9:00 p.m., she now considered herself a smart, savvy person who could stay up past 2:00 in the morning and still get up for an 8:30 a.m. class.

And sex with Christopher was incredible! Even though she had been married for more than fifteen years, Lauren had been a sexual innocent when she met Christopher. She discovered that she had a sexual appetite that added to her feeling of becoming a new woman. Sex and alcohol made a heady and potent mixture.

She moved in with Christopher. His friends liked her, and all seemed well. She loved being a part of a group of educated people who stayed up late drinking and discussing world politics. Soon she was able to hold her own in the conversations and able to keep up with all the drinking.

Everyone drank, but Christopher, with Lauren matching him, seemed to do the majority of the drinking. The alcohol added to the fun, or so Christopher said. His friends seemed to agree that Chris became more passionate after he had been drinking. In fact, his buddies privately refer to Christopher's earnest professor's voice as his "whino-voice" because, as one of them said, "Chris *whines* when he drinks wine!"

Lauren knew Christopher drank a lot, but he was a professorial type, a passionate man who needed to unwind. Christopher depended on Lauren in a way that her ex never had. She accepted that. Life with Christopher was exciting and novel. He always asked her to "pick up a few bottles" on her way home from her last class. Christopher had taught her well about what to buy, and Lauren, knowing how much he could consume in one night, always made sure his liquor cabinet was full.

Drinking became their nightly ritual. On their own Lauren and Christopher could easily drink a bottle or a bottle and a half of wine each.

After the wine, maybe some scotch, a little liqueur; all were everyday occurrences. Nights were spent in a boozy haze.

Besides being his lover and companion, Lauren found she was also becoming a sort of therapist to Christopher. The alcohol brought out mood swings that were upsetting. He was sometimes a cruel, vicious man, angry at the world and screaming his torment at her. Or, almost worse, an emotional wreck, sobbing over a career he felt was stagnating. She helped him through all the moods and drank with him even when she knew it was the booze that was causing the moods.

Eventually the consumption of alcohol began to get in the way of everyday life. While Christopher could and did go to classes after heavy drinking, Lauren was having a problem with all the booze. There were days when she was so hung over that she missed classes. She was forgetting to do assignments, and her grades began to suffer. Her student counselor told her she was in danger of failing several courses and wanted to know what was wrong. Lauren left thinking that maybe next semester she would do better. Once she got herself together, she'd be okay.

But she knew that she was letting herself down once again, and that was hard to take.

Lauren's appearance changed. She began to get the bloated look and flushed face of a habitual drinker. When she glanced in the mirror before leaving for classes, she couldn't see any of her former prettiness. That made her so sad she poured herself a drink before going out the door, promising herself this would be her last one.

But there was worse to come.

Booze, Battles, and Blackouts

A major problem was that the couple were beginning to fight when they were drinking—fights that were becoming more and more physical. The next day neither one of them could remember what had started the arguments, only the anger that had been fueled by the booze. Still, it was what it was. It was just the way they lived. And the make-up sex was almost worth the fights.

But that way of living for Lauren ended one night when she knew that the drinking had gone way too far. They had both gotten very drunk. Besides the wine, they had consumed half a bottle of scotch. They fought viciously. In the heat of anger and alcohol, Lauren shoved Christopher hard away from her. He fell in the dining room and didn't get up. Unable to rouse him, Lauren feared he was dead. She was ashamed and afraid to call for help because of her own drunken state. But Christopher wasn't moving. Terrified, Lauren finally made herself call a close friend of Chris who came over, checked him, and said, "He's okay, Lauren. Just passed out drunk. Don't worry, you're lucky, he won't remember any of this in the morning. He gets blackouts."

That night, too dazed to do anything else, Lauren fell asleep on the floor near Christopher. The following afternoon, after having missed her morning classes yet again due to a devastating hangover, she dragged herself out for coffee. Things had to change.

Lauren knew that she wanted a different life than the one she was living with Christopher. Alcohol was interfering too much with her planned goals. She remembered one night when she was in a lecture hall where the professor talked well past the time for class to end. Glancing at the wall clock every few minutes, she was itching to get out of there. The need to get to the liquor store before it closed was urgent. She and Christopher wouldn't be able to get through the night without it. What was most telling about that statement was the word *need*. It put drinking on the same level as breathing, and she knew that she had to stop what she was doing or it would possess her life.

Her marriage had had many problems, but alcohol and violence weren't among them. She saw that her consumption of alcohol was consuming her life, a life she had painstakingly created after her divorce. She had postponed college once when she had gotten married; she couldn't afford to do it for the second time.

Changing *You* Won't *Change* Him

Needing and willing to make a change, Lauren waited for almost a month before she talked with Christopher about their drinking. She still brought home the alcohol but seriously wanted to stop the nightly boozing. It was affecting her grades, and she had worked too hard to give up her goal of finally getting a degree. Moving out of Chris's apartment seemed to be the best thing for her at the moment. Her drinking was completely out of hand. If she didn't leave she would lose everything.

Christopher agreed with her that *she* needed to cut back on her drinking, but it wasn't necessary for her to move out; he *needed* her to stay. When Lauren gently mentioned that Christopher might want to address *his* drinking habits, he was surprised. He told her that he was able to function with alcohol, it didn't affect him the way it did her.

"But you have blackouts, Christopher. You're becoming violent toward me. Doesn't that scare you? Don't you think you have a problem?"

"It *enhances* my thinking," he told her. "I'm an intellectual. All the great philosophers were drinkers to an extent. You might not be able to handle one or two drinks the way the rest of us can."

But she knew that it wasn't that she couldn't handle "one or two drinks"; what she couldn't handle was drinking to excess.

Lauren went to campus counseling and began to see that staying with Christopher for the rest of the school year was not going to help her change. There was a large amount of drinking going on with him and his friends just about every night; if she stayed, she would continue to be a part of it.

"By drinking with Christopher, you are both an enabler as well as alcohol-addicted," a counselor told her. "Right now, you need to focus on curing yourself before you can help someone else."

She agreed she couldn't focus on helping them both. For the next three months, though she made frequent trips to the liquor store for Christopher, Lauren knew it was almost over. Finally she made her decision to leave. She needed to concentrate on her original goal of finishing her degree and making a new life for herself. First, though, Lauren had to heal herself. She made the choice to help herself, and it was the right one.

Though she wanted to stay with him and help him realize what he was doing to himself before it was too late, Lauren moved out of Christopher's apartment and rented a room in a private home. She had failed one class, had low grades in her others, and was put on academic probation for the next semester. Her counselor told her she had been in real danger of losing her scholarship. Lauren had had enough of "the art of drinking." It had almost destroyed her.

AN ENABLER NO MORE

Beth was one woman who had had enough of being hurt, fearful, and supporting a man in his drug habit. She knew that by staying with Daniel, she was putting her life in danger and running the real risk of police action against her as an accomplice if drugs were ever found in her condo or car. She also knew that life with Daniel would be a life of fear. Fear of losing him to an overdose, fear of other drug addicts, fear of losing her own life. And she couldn't, and wouldn't, live with fear. But even while she was leaving, she couldn't quite forgive herself for abandoning Daniel.

Lauren was dazzled by Christopher's sophistication and saw his drinking as part of his charm. She was willing to postpone her degree, something she had done before, in order to be a part of this man's life. Her decision almost cost her everything she was working to achieve. Leaving the circle of friends who saw drinking as a normal part of existence was the best thing she could have done for herself.

An addict and an enabler are a toxic mix. So are two addicts living together. As soon as addiction enters a relationship, the poisoning begins, and few couples survive it. Don't believe that your relationship will be one of the few. Chances are good that it won't. There is no sugarcoating this situation. Unless there is a firm commitment from the addict to seek help and end the addiction immediately, the enabler should not hesitate to leave.

As an enabler you are part of a combustible relationship. Your love and financial support are allowing him to be the way he is. You are giving him the permission and the means to stay an addict. Subconsciously as an enabler you are blinded by your strong feelings for the addict and hope that by being understanding and taking care of him, you will change his behavior. What you fail to realize is that you are being cleverly played by a man whose next fix or high means more to him than you ever will. It is a disease, but it is one that the addict will seek to have no matter what you do for him.

TOXIC COUPLE: THE KEYS TO SAVING YOURSELF

Get counseling.

You need counseling. You are as much, or in some cases more, a victim of the addict's problem as he is. A counselor will help you understand that leaving him is the only option for a healthy life. Even if you feel you can cope with leaving on your own, you need to remember that you had a hard time coping with the original issue of being part of a toxic couple.

Counseling helps.

A counselor can give you a detached perspective on the situation and what you are going through. He or she can help you face the hard facts of your decision and suggest ways for you to cope and begin a new life. Your therapist can help you understand why you might be attracted to the type of man who has an addictive personality and give you some pointers on not repeating your mistakes in the future.

Cancel the guilt trip—you are not to blame.

A woman who is living with an addict or alcoholic can easily feel that his addiction is somehow her fault. It is a mothering role. Subconsciously, you feel that his habit reflects badly on you personally, as if you didn't do enough to prevent this from happening to him. Understand that *it* didn't just happen; he actively pursued addiction. Addicts are adept at placing the blame for their addiction on everyone except themselves. Don't fall for it. An addict becomes one by choice. No matter how sad the circumstances, it was still *his* personal choice. Unless you brought the drugs home and force-fed them to him, you are not to blame. But you need to understand that while his addiction is not your *fault,* it has become your *problem.*

It is a similar story with an alcoholic. Alcoholics do not see their drinking as a problem They can handle it, they function better after drinking; you're the one who has a problem! This is especially true if you are joining them in their drinking. Before you begin to believe this, you have to take a different path and leave. If you are both an enabler and an addict, your priority is to get help for yourself first. You can help no one unless you do this.

Forgive yourself . . . and heal.

Even though Beth knew deep down that she wasn't to blame for Daniel's addiction, she had misplaced guilt. This is human emotional nature. The person you find hardest to forgive comes as no surprise. It is you. Not forgiving yourself for failing to help someone whose problem is beyond your control is fruitless. Forgiveness of self is a necessary part of healing any damage in your past. Lauren was terrified at how close she came to flunking out of school and never being able to get the degree that meant so much to her. Her guilt was tinged with anger at herself. By drinking with Christopher, she had become an enabler and an addict.

Take enough time to begin your life anew.

Any traumatic situation you have survived in your life will take recovery time. Give yourself plenty of time before you think about dating again. Take at least a year to settle your life and have some "alone time" to consider what you've been through and how you will improve your life. This is the time to be good to yourself. You need to get out of any negative relationships that stifle your capacity to be happy. Negativity begets negativity. Don't tell yourself that any relationship is better than no relationship at all. If the partnership is making you wish the days away, take steps to end it. It is okay to be a little selfish. In fact, a little selfishness is a healthy and necessary ingredient to be happy.

Make sure to learn from your past.

You need to move on from the past, absolutely. But you need to make sure that you've learned something important about yourself and what you want in a relationship. Realize how very much any relationship can impact your life for good or bad. Write down, in detail, what you expect from a partner—and write down what you will definitely not accept. It has been said before, but it needs to be repeated: This is real life, not a movie with a happy ending where your love changes a "bad" man. If you are willing to live that fantasy, you will be waiting for a happy ending that never comes.

Reality is not all bad. In fact, it shows you what your options are and the truth about what you are capable of doing with your life. You are in charge of what you do.

TOXIC COUPLES 101: LESSONS LEARNED

A word about potentially toxic relationships. You pretty much know if you're involved in one. Your gut instinct doesn't lie. A few can be saved, but you need to think about the following before deciding if yours is worth the effort without being harmful to you.

If what you once had was a really good situation, a loving relationship that included respect and kindness, then saving it makes sense.

It is a rare couple who experience no upsetting problems in their relationship at least once in their lives together. However, damage can be repaired only if both partners are willing to work together. Addiction is a time bomb; addicts are the first to admit they are never cured. They call themselves "recovering addicts." Are you able and willing to live with the risk? Knowing the good you had and longing to have it again, albeit with a more mature knowledge of each other, is a clear indication that your relationship is important to you. Working together to rebuild your life is key to being successful as a couple. You can overcome the small bumps in the road. Life-damaging problems, however, are not small bumps. But what if your relationship has always been a bit rocky and gotten progressively so as the years have passed? Are you the only partner who wants to save the relationship?

If drug or alcohol abuse has escalated to a danger point, are you still willing to still see the relationship as salvageable? Some people hold on to a relationship and a partner out of fear: fear of being alone, financial fear, and fear of the unknown life outside of being a couple. If any of these are your main reasons for trying to save a partnership that is not healthy or good for you, seek counseling to help you overcome your fears and advise you on what you can do to transition to a new life. Living with fear and an unhappy relationship will take a tremendous toll on your mental and physical health.

What if you're sexually compatible, and the sexual part of your relationship leaves you totally breathless? All right, that *is* a hard part of life to give up, I agree. But as hard as it is to believe when you're "in the moment," sex is another way that addicts and alcoholics keep a damaged relationship going. The so-called make-up sex, the "I'll change, I really will, please don't leave me" sex is so good that sometimes it's all you can remember about bad times.

Yet as good as it is, sex alone should not be the basis of your life as a couple. If you were *only* having sex with this person and living a very separate day-to-day life on your own, if you didn't see yourself as part of a couple with him, it would be different. A separate life with him on the side might work. But if you're living together, not a chance.

It all comes down to whether you have more negative than positive aspects in your relationship. If you do, then keep the hot memories as a part of the best part—possibly the only good part—of the relationship, and let it end. The sex alone will not be worth the sacrifices you will be forced to make in every other area of your life with him.

Not all relationships are worth saving; some have to be dissolved so that people can get on to a new healthier, happier life. The bottom line is how you see the relationship in terms of the effects it has on your quality of life. Any relationship where abuse is ongoing or where the other person's addiction is adversely affecting your life is a relationship not worth saving.

When a relationship does need *saving*, it usually has taken quite a hit and is sorely damaged. Whether it is damaged beyond repair is an individual call. Trying to save a relationship takes as much time and effort as building one. You have to ask yourself just how much of your days and nights you are willing to spend to save what you once had. Only you can be the judge. Judge well; this is *your* life.

CHAPTER 7

○— The Key to Allowing
Your Dreams to Become
┡ Your Plans
When Someday Never Comes

Ah, time! When we are younger, it seems infinite. We always seem to have an endless vista of days, weeks, months, years. We can suspend our happiness, for others, for work, for anything, so absolutely certain are we that whatever it is we want, we're sure to get it "someday." Thinking about someday isn't totally wrong. Certainly everyone has an idea of an event such as a graduation, a job, or a wedding that is going to take place in the future. You think about it, you plan it, and you have every intention of fulfilling that dream. The problem with someday comes when you allow too many obstacles to be placed in the way of achieving your goal. You can waste a lifetime dreaming about someday and never have it come unless you make your dreams into solid plans. Caren is one woman who allowed too many obstacles to stand in the path to her dream.

CAREN'S STORY
Caren was planning to study in Italy "someday." She loved all things Italian: the culture, the language, the architecture, but most especially the art and literature of the

Renaissance. To live in Italy had been her dream since the age of thirteen. She would move to Florence after college and study there for a few years. She daydreamed about it constantly; she took classes in Italian all through school and became quite fluent. It was a definite in her mind. Someday in the future, someday; some happy day.

Her parents smiled indulgently at their daughter whenever she mentioned living in Italy. Caren was a dreamer, they thought. Look at how she had wanted to be an Italian Renaissance art history major! Her parents had had to convince her to major in marketing, a field that was more practical and not as chancy a career. She took a minor in art history.

Caren never forgot her dream. As graduation was approaching, she made plans for her move to Florence. When she told her parents that she would be leaving in the summer, her father was surprised but was willing to support his daughter in what she wanted to do. Her mother's reaction was altogether different. She began a nonstop campaign to keep Caren from going.

Her mother had never lived anywhere alone. She had gone to a local college, living in her parents' house until she was married. The fact that Caren lived in a college dorm that was three hours away from home gave her nightmares. She told Caren how very worried she would be if she went to live in a foreign country at the young age of twenty-two.

"You'll be in a strange country all alone. I'll go crazy with worry. You're still a baby in many ways. Wait a few years. You also need to get a good job. Get established in a solid company first. Do it for me, please."

Though she felt badly that her mother was so upset, Caren still wanted to pursue her dream. She had gone to college and gotten her degree in marketing as her parents had wanted; now *she* wanted a few years to be a post-grad student living in Italy before looking for a full-time job. She also wanted to pursue her interest in art history.

But her mother kept up the pressure, and she got help from the man her daughter was dating. She knew Caren was deeply involved with this man, hoping to become engaged in a few years. She was sure he would help in her campaign. She was right.

Caren's boyfriend was not happy that she would be leaving. It was out of the question that he go with her—he had been accepted into a graduate program. He wanted her to postpone her trip for a few years. Between her mother and her boyfriend, the pressure *not* to go was enormous. Even her dad, who secretly applauded what she wanted to do, hesitantly sided with her mother.

Very reluctantly, and a bit angry with herself for not doing what she wanted, Caren gave in. She wanted to be fair to her mother and boyfriend. They were only concerned for her.

Though she was disappointed, she thought there would be plenty of time to study in Italy in a few years. She placed her dream in the future. She was only twenty-two, after all. Caren was optimistic.

When she found an apartment an hour away and moved out, her mother did not utter one word of protest. It was a sort of consolation prize she offered to Caren for having prevented her from going to Italy. Caren felt as if she had scored a small victory.

Life had more changes in store for Caren. The boy-friend who had begged her not to go abroad without him suddenly ended their relationship after grad school and moved to the opposite coast. After having had such an influence over her life that he was partially to blame for preventing her trip to Italy, he didn't even try to maintain a relationship with her.

But Caren wasn't bitter or angry at his decision to leave, even though she had hoped their relationship was going to be a permanent one. Wiser and more mature, she decided to focus on beginning her adult life.

Caren had an optimistic attitude that she was going to accomplish whatever she set out to do. A few minor road-blocks seemed to be nothing that would keep her from doing what she had heart set on. Italy would be there and so would she, sometime in the future.

With a new apartment came a position in a company where competition was fierce among the new interns. Italy was put on hold once more while Caren worked hard to establish herself in her job. It was good that she loved what she did because the hours were long and she had little free time. She still dreamed about living in Italy for at least two years and studying art history. So she had to wait a couple of years—what's two years to a twenty-five-year-old? Her hard work paid off, and at thirty she had her own office with her name plate on the door.

And there was still plenty of time to go study in Italy.

Postponing Your Life

Caren began saving for her own house, which took finan-cial priority over going to Italy. At thirty-two she married, had children soon after, and worked her way into a position of high respect at her office, still thinking about her dream of studying in Italy. What with an important job, marriage, and children, however, she postponed it once again. Her dream was out there in the future just waiting for her. A couple of years down the road, she'd only be in her forties. Forty is not old; it's the new thirty, right? There's plenty of time.

Happiness is . . .
. . . being in charge of your life.
Live life with a purpose. Don't drift aimlessly; have an eye on the horizon and know where you're going and what your true goal is.

After a while Caren created a thought pattern about going to Italy that she repeated over and over in her head. Someday, someday when she felt freer to do as she liked, someday when she had money that didn't have to be spent on other things, someday when she had more time, someday when no one depended on her, someday . . .

As the years passed, her someday was pushed farther and farther into the future. Motherhood, a hostile divorce, her demanding job with long hours, all delayed Caren's dream of happiness. She was exhausted but financially set.

Caren finally made plans. When her children were both in college, she would spend a year in Florence and study art history. This time it would be written in stone; nothing and no one would prevent her from giving herself this gift. Her fifties would be the decade of a new beginning.

Caren planned to go to Italy during the summer of her fifty-second year. Plane reservations were made, she had rented an apartment in Florence, classes at the University of Florence had been scheduled, her college-aged children would take care of her house; everything was set. All Caren had to do was leave.

Around the time of her fifty-second birthday, Caren began having shortness of breath and a tight feeling in her jaw and neck. Sometimes simply walking up the stairs left her completely winded. She put it down to the stresses related to her daily life and pretty much ignored it. After all, she was going to Italy in two months!

When she collapsed at her office and was rushed to the hospital, it was discovered that Caren had had several "silent" but significant heart attacks. There was sufficient damage to her heart and enough blockage in her arteries that she had to undergo major surgery. Recovery, said her doctor, would be long. She was stunned.

Caren's dream of studying in Italy hadn't come true. She had to leave her well-paying job because of the enormous amount of stress involved. She almost lost her life and felt debilitated and weak. Having always taken superb health for granted, she went through a period of depression at being limited in what she could do. Her children clung to her because they had almost lost her and were afraid to let her out of their sight. Her mother said it was a miracle she hadn't gone to Italy; she might have died far away from home.

Traveling abroad no longer seemed viable. She was afraid of having another heart attack, this time in a foreign country. Her dream had been postponed so many times that now it would be almost impossible to live it. The ironic part of this story is a statement her father made when he came to visit, bringing her a new book on Italian Renaissance artists.

"You should have taken that year off and gone to Italy after college. Your mother was wrong to stop you, and I was wrong to let her. It's a shame you didn't do what you wanted to do when you were twenty. It was your dream. You should have eaten your ice cream while it was still on the plate."

Hearing her father make that wistful statement relit the spark that had always shone in Caren. It was the words *should have* that made the difference. *Should, could, can, will*—she began to seriously rethink her options in life. Before it was too late, before her "ice cream" melted, she had to make her dreams into her plans.

•••

Getting lost in day-to-day life can also make sure your own "someday" never comes. The next story shows that all too well.

KIMBERLY'S STORY

Kimberly's story was a little different from that of Caren. Kimberly didn't quite know exactly how to get back to what she had once had. She only knew she wasn't happy with the life she was living. It wasn't a bad life, it just wasn't how she had thought her life would turn out. She'd had plans but marriage and children had postponed them. Being a wife and a mother wasn't all she wanted, though. She needed more.

Kimberly went to work right out of a two-year college. She was in the field of technology and she loved her job. Her career was fun, interesting, and fulfilling.

At twenty-four she met and fell in love with a nice guy who had a well-paying job. He had had a great education and his professional career was very promising. They made plans to marry.

During the engagement Kimberly told him about her hopes for the future and how very important it was to her to continue her career. Her field was constantly changing, and taking classes would always be a major part of her job. Her fiancé tried to be understanding about what she wanted to do but he didn't understand the need she had "for a career." He asked only that she take a year off when they had a child. That was important to him. They both agreed that having children would be quite a few years in the future.

Happiness isn't...

... being complacent and not focusing on goals. It doesn't mean that you give up striving for what you do want. It doesn't mean you are giving up. It simply means that while you are not where you want to be, you are still working toward your future goals.

When they'd been married eight months, Kimberly discovered that she was pregnant. She hadn't wanted a child so soon—in fact, they had discussed waiting at least five years before starting a family. But her husband was thrilled. He told her that he wanted a "houseful of kids," and his enthusiasm rubbed off on Kimberly. She felt a little more at ease about becoming a mother and left her job temporarily when the baby was born.

At first it was fun staying home with her child. Her daughter was such a good baby that she even thought about returning to work earlier than she had planned. But a second pregnancy followed rather quickly. Kimberly soon found herself a stay-at-home mom with two children under the age of three and very limited time for herself.

She made the choice to stay home rather than have the babies put in a day care center. She felt that children under the age of five should have the security of a full-time parent. Kim would've have liked her husband to take parental leave for a year, but that was out of the question. His career was too important for him to even consider it.

Kimberly was a bit jealous of him. She had had a promising career, too.

In a couple of years, she seemed to have a good life. They even moved into the proverbial house in the suburbs with the white picket fence. Her husband's income made life very comfortable. He thought that life for them was perfect. It may have seemed that way for him—but not so much for Kimberly.

Lost in Day-to-Day Life

With his career really taking off, Kimberly's husband wanted her to be a mom who didn't work outside the home; she certainly didn't need to. He had come from a family where his mother hadn't worked after her children were born, and he wanted the same for his children. He convinced her that since she was taking time off to raise the two they already had, why not have a third?

"My salary is more than enough for our family. You don't have to work, Kim. Stay home, at least for now. The time isn't right for you to have a career."

A little reluctantly, and feeling like a brood mare, Kimberly agreed. After all, why not? Then she'd have it over with and could get on with what she had planned to do. Right now everything was on hold anyway.

In her most frustrated moments, Kim felt that there had to be time for her somewhere down the road. In a few years when the kids were in school, she just assumed she'd be happy doing what she had always planned to do. Right now it was better to get lost in day-to-day life and go along with the flow.

The truth was that if you'd asked Kimberly if she was happy, she would have immediately answered, "Yes, of course. Why wouldn't I be?" But there was always that small feeling in her mind that she wasn't happy. Not really. She didn't want to admit this to anyone but, for her, motherhood wasn't all that fulfilling. Kimberly thought that other women might think she was a terrible mother if she voiced her thoughts. But she couldn't deny her true feelings to herself. She did not enjoy being a stay-at-home mother. When a colleague told her that her old job, the one she had loved and to which she had always planned to return, was being filled by someone new, Kimberly felt a deep sadness.

She resigned herself to just drifting along and left her happiness out there in the future because, of course, it *would* be there. It *had* to be there someday. As her husband said, now was not the right time.

The years went by, and so did Kimberly's life. Her family made up the core of her daily existence. Day followed uneventful and slightly boring day. It wasn't that she didn't love her children and want the best for them; she did. But the car-pooling, the volunteering at schools, the incessant "mommy talk" from other women about nothing but children, school, cleaning, and cooking left her disappointed and frustrated. There were times she wanted to scream, she was so bored by the mindless routine of her life.

When she discussed her feelings with her husband, he was surprised at the way she felt. His own mother had loved being home and not having to work! What was wrong with Kimberly?! Good mothers stay home. He said as much to her, and Kimberly began to think that maybe the fault *was* within her! Still, she knew her own feelings.

When her three children were in school full-time, Kimberly contacted her former employer. Her work history was ten years old and she hadn't kept up with new advances in her field, so returning to what she'd done before was out. However, a new position was being created that would require a couple of months of classes for tech training. If she was really interested in returning, the position was hers, but the company had to know soon. She had a week to decide.

Kimberly was excited. She was finally going to get back to a semblance of the work life she loved. She told her husband what she planned to do—but he wasn't happy.

"The greatest job in the world is being a wife and mother. Aren't you happy with that? Can't you wait until the kids are out of school? Now is not the right time."

But she wasn't happy and she couldn't wait. If she waited she would lose a vital part of her own self, the part that needed more than being a wife and mother could fulfill.

Kimberly told him, "I've *already* waited too long. If I don't do this, I will have missed a great career opportunity. I have to do it now. Now *is* the right time."

Dreams versus "What You're Supposed to Do"

Caren did everything she was "supposed" to do in life, yet the one thing she actually wanted to do didn't happen until it was almost too late. It took her more than two years before she felt well enough to go to Italy. During that time she worked on getting healthy and planned the minutest details of the year she would be spending abroad. She would be near a university hospital.

Since stairs still made her breathless, she chose a first-floor apartment and requested a live-in housekeeper. Her classes at a small art college were mornings only so she'd have the afternoons to rest. When her mother voiced her fears and anxiety again about Caren having another heart attack and possibly dying so far away from everyone, Caren, aided by her father, told her mother that she was going no matter what.

"If anything is going to happen to me, it can just as well happen here as there. My dreams are becoming my plans now. I can't be afraid."

Her children had been told how important this trip was to their mother, and they were extremely supportive. One of her daughters planned to join her in Italy for two weeks in the spring. Caren would finally live her dream. It frightened her to think how close she had come to never having it come true. She realized that every opportunity should be taken in order to live a full and satisfying life. Years can melt away without you ever having enjoyed the moments simply because everything wasn't perfect.

Kimberly had to take the initiative and make known her needs for what would fulfill her. Despite the persistent—but erroneous—belief that motherhood is the greatest fulfillment women can know, there are a great many women who do not feel this way at all. It is wrong to think that simply because you don't wholeheartedly enjoy staying home to be a mother, there is something "wrong" with you. There isn't. That is a myth. While being a mother is one of the most beautiful experiences many women have, there is still a desire for a more personal expression of self. Apple pie and mom are not for every woman.

Happiness is . . .

. . . living in the moment but planning for the future. Living in the moment may sound like a New Age cliché, but there is a real kernel of truth in it. Being aware of life is your window to the world.

The great writer Oscar Wilde told a friend how he had survived his two years in prison. He said he had the gift of a small window that was located near the ceiling of his cell. While his cellmate totally disregarded that small patch of light, Oscar Wilde saw it as a precious gift to keep him alive in the moment. Through that window, he watched the sky change colors, watched the seasons revolve, and observed the stars and moon in the dark night while he made plans for his life after prison. No matter how dreary his prison was, he was able to survive by focusing on his goals.

Telling her husband that now was the right time for her to return to a career was the only way for Kimberly to make him understand that she would no longer adhere to his ideas on how she should live. Had she listened to him and postponed her career yet again, the time would never have been right for her to return to it. What he didn't understand was that she needed more than motherhood to validate her as a person.

Doing what you want and need to do is a simple case of prioritizing what is important to you personally. A fulfilling life is lived by placing wants and needs in a specified order of importance. Make plans and make a timetable for them.

PRIORITIZE YOUR LIFE, DON'T POSTPONE IT. THE KEYS FOR YOUR PRIORITY LIST

Be your own manager.

A good manager takes the opinions of others into consideration when making an important decision. Then she listens to her own counsel and does what she thinks is best. Make an executive decision concerning your life that will benefit you the most. While the idea of being the manager of your own life may seem a no-brainer, you would be surprised at how many women fail at the job. They may be successful in business, the field of medicine or law, or in any other job, but managing their own lives is difficult. Why?

We are certainly influenced by those around us, especially those with whom we are close. Their suggestions, their fears, their attitudes about everything from food to travel make an impression on us in ways we don't even realize. Unfortunately, we sometimes mistake their ideas as the ones that are best for our own lives, even if we do so begrudgingly. You are not your mother, your grandmother, your husband, your boyfriend, your best friend, or anyone else who exerts a strong influence on you. Their ideas and experiences about life differ vastly from yours. Their decisions are based on what *they* know and what they have learned. You owe them only the courtesy of listening to them, nothing more.

Make managing your life a conscious effort that puts forward your own ideas about what path will reap you the most rewards emotionally.

Chart your course and stick to it no matter what.

Plan, plan, plan! Nothing important gets done without careful planning. Be positive in your outlook about what you want to do. Don't allow anyone or anything to stop you from doing what you feel in your heart is right. Being assertive will win out every time against the negative opinions of others. Your goals will not just happen without effort. Life is a planned strategy.

Give yourself some wiggle room but . . .

Sometimes you may have to change the path to achieving your life's dream. That's okay; adjustments in time or circumstances can be made. The key is to never endlessly postpone your plans. Time itself may be endless, but your own time is not. Being flexible doesn't mean stopping what you plan to do. It means being ready to make small changes in those plans that won't affect them in any crucial way.

Don't capitulate, negotiate . . . wisely.

How important is your dream to you? Seriously consider how you will feel if you decided to *never* attempt to fulfill your dream. What effect would this have on your quality of life, your attitude, your future, and your happiness?

Some accommodations are an inevitable part of life, but denying yourself what you want simply to appease others is not an accommodation—it is a capitulation and a waste of potential. Small accommodations and sacrifices are sometimes a necessary part of negotiations, but they should not have the power to stop you in your tracks.

Be a savvy person and negotiate in your favor.

Allow your dreams to become your plans.

Caren had the correct answer to her mother's fear about her living in a foreign country and the possibility of another heart attack occurring so far from home:

"My dreams are becoming my plans. I can't be afraid."

Being afraid to live your dream is an acknowledgment that you are only existing. Healthy concern should always outweigh outright fear in your life. No one is exempt from fear, but allowing fear to rule your mind and life is unhealthy. If you always give in to fear, you may need to speak with a therapist who will help you understand why you are consistently afraid.

Concern is practical and normal; we'd be fools to be concerned about nothing. Fear, however, can be paralyzing. Never be fearful of living your life the way you want. Be fearful instead of coming to the end of your life with nothing to remember but regrets and "could-haves."

Kimberly got lost in daily living and was never content to stay home. Filling her husband's image of what a good mother should be was wrong for her. There are all types of good mothers. Some work outside the home, some do not. Some travel for work, others don't. Neither one is the better mother. There is no one definition.

You cannot live your own life by another's idea of how your role should be played. You need your own interpretation of the role and to act in whatever way is best for you.

EAT YOUR ICE CREAM BEFORE IT MELTS 101: LESSONS LEARNED

A child doesn't have to be told to eat her ice cream; she's so caught up in the moment of happiness that the ice cream is all she can see. And you had better believe that no one should attempt to take that ice cream away from her! She will put up a terrific fight to keep it!

Add the fact that the dish the ice cream comes in doesn't really matter. A child only anticipates the pleasure of the ice cream. The bowl doesn't have to be perfect for her to savor the taste of what is in it. She looks forward to it, and when she gets that bowl of ice cream in front of her, she eats it immediately. If she didn't do this, if she simply waited for the "right time" to eat it, she'd be left with a melted mess. A child knows this and doesn't hesitate to be happy with the ice cream in front of her. It is the moment that counts, not what came before and certainly not what comes after.

What happens to women as adults? Why do we feel that we must wait for the perfect time and conditions to eat our "ice cream?" Why do we let it melt away while we cater to the whims of others?

We allow this to happen in our lives. Wait too long for the perfect time for happiness and all your years will melt away. Life is not a dress rehearsal, and happiness is not a set of perfect conditions. It is not a place or time that you will ever get to experience simply by waiting. It is a right-here, right-now situation.

The future won't automatically be magically perfect. It relies pretty heavily on what you do today. Each experience that you allow or don't allow leads you to your future self.

CHAPTER 8

The Key to Surviving an Affair
He's Married . . . But Not to You

Being part of any couple can be challenging and unpredictable, as we all know. But when the man with whom you're involved is part of *another* couple, someone else's husband, then the challenge and unpredictability can make your life a messy, unhappy waiting game that you will rarely win.

The woman who is in love with a married man lives a life that, for the most part, is shrouded in secrecy. Her close circle of friends might know about her affair, but she really cannot let anyone else, such as colleagues or her family, know. She is alone most of the time and spends it waiting: waiting for her married lover to call, to come meet her, to share some precious time together. She is not his wife, she is not mother to his children, she is not his parents' daughter-in-law. Her chance for happiness hinges on a future that is highly uncertain to say the least.

JENNA'S STORY

"I love him." This was always Jenna's heartfelt answer when her friends questioned her about being involved with a married man. "You can't help who you fall in love with."

Her friends were never judgmental, just concerned about how Jenna chose to live. "Alone" seemed to be her middle name. She was alone on weekends, alone on holidays, took vacations alone, and attended weddings alone. She canceled any and all plans she may have made for herself whenever Denis called. And then there were too many times when, after she had canceled *her* plans with friends so she could be with him, he called and said *he* couldn't make it after all. His excuse was always "family obligations."

"Doesn't that bother you at all? That he calls and cancels?" asked a friend.

"Not at all, his family comes first, at least right now. I accept that." And Jenna truly believed that she did accept it at the present time.

She didn't tell her friends what Denis had told her: that when his children were older, he would file for divorce; that his marriage was only one of convenience for the children's sake; that Jenna was his whole life and that he wanted her to wait for him to "be free."

She didn't tell them that she dreamed about marrying Denis and being a sophisticated, kindhearted stepmother to his three daughters. She would have them over for holidays and weekends, take them shopping, never daring to try to replace their mother, just happy to be a loving older friend whom they would come to adore. She and Denis and his three girls would be a modern, happy stepfamily.

Jenna had been with Denis for six years, and the first three had been magical. They had met when he had come into the bookstore she owned to find an out-of-print children's book for his daughter's birthday. She had the book but she was so impressed by Denis's good looks and his shy smile when he talked about his oldest daughter, and her love of reading, that she told him she had to order it; he could pick it up in a couple of days.

She wanted to see him again.

And see him again she did. After buying the book, Denis asked her to have a late lunch with him as a thank-you for having gotten him the book his daughter wanted so much. Jenna accepted. It was to be the first of many lunches, dinners, and meetings for drinks the two of them would share.

Denis also made it a habit at least twice a week to stop in her bookstore to "just talk." He always brought coffee and hot scones from a gourmet shop for both of them. While they drank the coffee, he would unburden himself about his unhappy marriage, his love for "my sweet little girls," and his sadness at how he was living a half life with a woman who didn't love him. But he was kind about his wife, always noting what a great mom she was and how he was sorry that their marriage wasn't all he had hoped it would be.

Jenna always listened intently and was very compassionate. This poor, unhappy man! Burdened with a loveless woman, only staying with his wife because he loved his girls so much and didn't want to leave them, trapped in a miserable life he hadn't ever expected. How courageous a man, how wonderful a father! With the smell of hazelnut crème coffee in the air and the gentle sound of his voice, Jenna fell deeply in love with Denis.

The first time they made love in her bedroom, Jenna felt conflicting emotions. She was in love with Denis, yes, but this man who lay in her arms *was* married to another woman—the mother of his children at that. How could she do this? Jenna wrestled with the thought. She wasn't religious and she didn't feel that what she had done was a "sin," but still . . . there was the question of morality and what was right. Why was loving someone so totally complicated? It should be simple. Even while she was thinking these thoughts, she knew she wanted to keep on seeing Denis and knew that intimacy would always be a part of their being together. What they had done that afternoon had been tender and sweet. Should she feel guilt over sleeping with another woman's husband? She had never done anything like this before.

Jenna felt some guilt about having a relationship with Denis, but more than that she felt a sense of uneasiness about who and what she was in his life. Being with a married man, what exactly would her status be? She didn't want to be the *other woman*. That term was not something she wanted to describe her. The old-fashioned term *mistress* was just ridiculous. And the word *affair* itself was too sordid for what she was getting into. She felt uneasy at what she was about to begin. What would her position be? What was she giving up to become someone who was merely a lady-in-waiting, a woman who would be living her life in the shadows, so to speak, and who had no real claim on Denis in any way except in her bed?

Then she thought about how unhappy Denis was and how he had said that his unhappiness stemmed from a marriage to a woman who, mother of his children or not, didn't love him at all. The thought of his wife not loving Denis won her internal argument, and Jenna embarked on an affair with a married man letting any qualms about morality drift away. Her love was a balm that would heal Denis.

The beginning of the affair was a heady and romantic period. Mostly they were content to stay in the bookstore or in Jenna's small house. Jenna was in love and thrilled that Denis said he felt the same way.

The Rules of the Affair

There were date rules, of course. One of them concerned Denis's fear of being found out. For example, when he came to her house he asked that the outside lights be turned off and the garage door open so he could drive his car into the garage without being seen.

They rarely went out, but when they did they were careful to go places where they wouldn't be seen by any of Denis's friends or colleagues. If they ate at a restaurant, they never arrived together, and Jenna didn't enter until Denis had checked to see who was there and made sure they would have a table in an obscure area. It was all mysterious and exciting.

Holidays were bittersweet; he always tried to sneak away for a few hours, but it was difficult. The rule here was that he would be the one to get in touch with her. *She* was never to try to reach *him*. It was the same when he went away on family vacations "for the girls' sake." No contact. Jenna contented herself with brief phone calls or text messages.

During the first three years, Denis talked about the future when his girls would be old enough to understand a divorce and to better handle the breakup of their parents. He intended to always be a strong and permanent presence in their lives and couldn't wait for the day that Jenna could also be a part of their world. He mentioned how he and his wife really had "no relationship at all," the only thing they shared was parenting, and Jenna believed he meant that there was no sexual relationship between them.

He earnestly told Jenna that next to his daughters, she was the most important person in his life, and he *hoped* they could have a life together. When he talked like that, Jenna basked in the daydreams. She didn't hear the word *hoped*.

Whenever her friends tried to fix her up with a "great unmarried guy," Jenna thought of what she would eventually have with Denis and always said no thank you, adding, "You don't understand what we have together and what we *will* have in the future."

Her friends just rolled their eyes and sighed.

The fourth year of the affair brought changes. As his girls got older, it was getting harder and harder for Denis to get away. The twice-weekly lovemaking sessions dropped down to one and then to once every two weeks. Going out was getting too risky; his oldest daughter was a teenager now, and you never knew where you might run into her or one of her friends.

Denis was a man who was genuinely in love with Jenna and trying to fit all the parts of his life together. He tried very hard to be understanding about her disappointment whenever he had to cancel their plans together, but he was becoming frustrated over the fact that Jenna didn't quite understand the responsibility of his life away from her. He was a father and a husband and there were obligations he had to meet. His time with his family and with Jenna was becoming more and more like a juggling act: He couldn't allow even one object to fall. Too many people were demanding a piece of his life. Something had to give.

Commitments made were often broken and Jenna was disappointed over and over again, waiting and hoping. His children had sports, his oldest daughter was going through a problem, his wife needed him to drive the girls to a party. It seemed he talked incessantly about his children, but now Jenna wasn't as interested in them as before; she felt they were taking him away from her.

Her friends still called with offers to set her up on dates with great single men they knew, but Jenna stubbornly clung to the idea that she and Denis had a future together. She told her friends that everything was going well. But there were problems in their relationship that she didn't tell them.

One was that Denis no longer talked about divorce. If Jenna mentioned their life together after he got his divorce, he became vague and a bit angry. Seeing his reaction, she became afraid to mention it at all. Another problem was that he was doing more and more things with his family, and those things included his wife. In fact, Jenna was surprised and jealous when he canceled a long-planned-for dinner with her because he had to visit a college over the weekend with his wife and daughter. His simple statement, "I'm sorry I have to cancel but we've been talking about this college for our daughter for quite some time," brought her to tears because this was something intimate he and his wife shared.

He went on to tell her that "their" daughter was one of the few prospective freshmen staying as a guest in a college dorm. He and his wife would be at a hotel nearby.

While Denis said all this matter-of-factly, just the thought that he and his wife would be staying in a hotel room together for the weekend hurt Jenna more than she ever thought it would. She was sure he wasn't going to sleep on a *couch* in that hotel room. The thought that he might have sex with his wife made her sick even while she realized that she had no right to feel that way.

Lonely Lady-in-Waiting

The affair was continuing, but there was a lack of excitement and passion in it now. Being alone 95 percent of the time was getting more difficult to take. Occasionally they still talked over coffee in the bookstore, but Jenna noticed that Denis was talking more and more about his life with his family. He no longer referred to his wife as the woman who was the cause of his unhappiness in a loveless marriage. *Now* she was a person who not only was a wonderful mother but who was going back to school to finish her master's degree. He was proud of her. *She* needed his support and guidance. Jenna couldn't help but feel jealous.

Yes, she Jenna was the "other woman," but hadn't she been the one who'd been there for Denis in his unhappiest moments? Hadn't she been the one who had comforted him with her love and her body? Did all her patience and sincere love mean nothing? Didn't he owe her more than to sit here talking with her about a woman whom he had said was ruining his life?

Jenna had once seen a picture of his wife. She hated herself for doing it but one night while he was in the shower she had checked his laptop. Going through his photo album, she saw pictures of his daughters snorkeling on a family vacation. In one of the pictures there was Denis with his arm around a pretty blond woman, laughing in the background.

She looked contented and relaxed, the way a woman looks when life is going well. The picture's caption read: "Mommy, Daddy, and the girls."

> ## Happiness isn't . . .
> . . . living on the edge of someone's life.
> A secretive relationship does not enhance your life; it takes away the opportunity to live happily.

Jenna knew she wasn't meant to see that picture and quickly put it away when she heard the shower stop.

Denis's visits became even more sporadic. Jenna had had nothing but text messages and e-mails—not even a phone call—for more than a month when Denis finally did call and asked to meet her in the bookstore. She had a dread that she couldn't explain, a dread she'd felt ever since he and his wife had gone together to look at a college for their daughter.

As soon as she saw his face, Jenna knew that this was to be their last time together. Denis had gotten to a place where he had had to make a hard choice about his life. He came to the point as soon as they sat down.

"Jenna, this is difficult for me, and I love you very much, but I can't be with you anymore. I'm trying very hard to make my marriage work. My wife and I have been married for twenty years and I owe it to her to give it my best effort. She's been a terrific mother and loyal to me. I know we can make our marriage work now."

Jenna was stunned. He "owed" the woman who had made his life miserable? What about what he owed *her*? Did what they had mean so little to him?

"You will always be in my heart, Jen, but we just can't be together anymore. My family and my wife need me now. I know you understand. You're strong and brave. There's some wonderful man out there for you, a good single man with no ties. He'll be lucky to get you. I'm so sorry, honey. I have no choice but to do this."

Jenna literally had nothing to say. He kissed her, both of them cried in each other's arms, and then he was gone. As quickly as he had come into her life, he left. All those years of him being there and now he was gone to be with his family. They needed him.

Now Jenna was 100 percent alone. She felt hurt, confused, and depressed.

The Painful Unwanted Truth

Denis wasn't a cruel man. He had genuine feelings for Jenna. She had come into his life when his marriage was in turmoil and she had helped him to cope. There may have been a time when he, too, fantasized about having a real life with Jenna and his daughters. He more than likely loved her and certainly didn't want to hurt her.

Unfortunately for Jenna, marriages go through many difficult stages, and most couples find a way to work through them no matter how long it takes. When the time came for Denis to choose between Jenna and his family, the choice in his mind was clear.

If she looked at it in hindsight, Jenna would have seen that the signs of the affair's ending had been there all along but she had refused to acknowledge them. Instinctively she had felt that being with Denis wouldn't last, but she didn't heed her gut feeling about what was happening right in front of her. A man who talks about his family and even his wife really has no intention of getting a divorce.

She began to wonder if he had left his laptop available hoping she would see that picture of him and his wife. Maybe he thought she might save him the trouble of having to be the one to break up.

Jenna also had gone into the affair knowing what her status would be, another fact she hadn't fully acknowledged. As hard as it is to accept, when you choose to be with a married man, the only role you can have is as "the other woman." All rights and privileges belong to his legal partner, his wife.

Accepting that his family will almost always come first may seem to be an easy thing to do, but it is not. You are only human, and the time will come when you develop a certain resentment toward your lover's family. This includes his children as well as his wife.

The key to finding your way is understanding your status in the affair. It is difficult for you to see the affair as simply a minor aspect of your own life because the man you are seeing and the time you spend together becomes the only life you know or want. Every other part of your life falls by the wayside. You are emotionally involved in ways that the man is not.

You need to step back and identify the priorities—*his* priorities, not yours—in a relationship with a married man. Here are the hard facts you need to know.

SURVIVING AN AFFAIR WITH A MARRIED MAN: THE KEYS TO WHAT YOU REALLY NEED TO KNOW

The needs of the many (namely, his family) will always outweigh your needs.
His family will always come first, and that includes his wife. Simply because he talks in a negative way about his marriage doesn't mean that his obligations to his wife are any less important to him. Whether or not they have children is a moot point; he will always feel as if he has to be a husband to her and take care of the marriage. Their life together includes friendships and a social network that is shared and comfortable for him. He *won't* risk losing that.

His life with you is secret and always will be.
No matter how much you may want to walk in the sunshine with him and have him openly acknowledge his love for you, it won't happen.

While he is more than willing to be your lover and to bring you gifts, he is not about to have you meet his friends and risk having his family find out about you.

No matter how nice a guy he is, you are a temporary diversion for him.
This is not an easy statement to comprehend. It's emotionally painful. Unfortunately it is true. The beginning of an affair is romantic and naughty at the same time. Planning to be together becomes a fascinating game and is thrilling to say the least. Stealing hours from work or home to have sex is exciting, and you may mistake his libido-driven

passion for undying love. Don't. The game soon becomes a chore for him, and romantic interludes are just one more thing he "has to do."

He will not leave his wife.

Less than 5 percent of men leave their wives for the woman with whom they are having an affair. Whether it is because of all the legal and financial problems attached to divorce or the fact that they have become comfortable with their marriage the way it is, or even because they still have a certain real love for their wives, men rarely end up with the other woman. And don't ever kid yourself on *this* important point: He *is* still having sex with his wife, no matter what you may want to believe.

Legally, financially, and emotionally, you have no claim.

You may realize that you have no claim legally or financially, but you would think there'd be an emotional attachment or bond between you and your lover. In fact there usually isn't after the affair is over. Here's why. Even though he has a deep feeling of love for you, he is able to process it in an unemotional way. He's not a bad guy, he may be a wonderfully kind person, but he is also a practical one. He knows that holding on to emotions that can only cause problems for his family is something he cannot and will not do. When it's over, he will move on.

SURVIVING THE AFFAIR 101: LESSONS LEARNED

Perhaps the best advice about having a relationship with a married man is the one telling you not to even start! However, that is not practical for all women. As Jenna said, "You can't help who you fall in love with." The love of your life just might be a married man.

To safeguard yourself from too much emotional pain, you need to understand that he can only be a small part of your life and will never be more than that no matter how many promises are made. You need to have a life that works and that is full enough to withstand the pain of the eventual breakup. He *has* one and you *need* one, too.

A solid circle of friends and a social life separate from your hidden life with him is a necessity. Let your friends know that you still want to go out with them regularly. Don't always be so ready to cancel plans you have made with others to accommodate him.

Casual dating with male friends helps, too. It allows you to see yourself through the eyes of another man who finds you interesting and attractive. It is up to you where it might lead. It helps to remember that the man with whom you are intimately involved in "your other life" is not living as a monk with his wife.

Being involved in an affair with someone else's husband is an almost surefire trip from ecstatic highs at the beginning to a depressing abyss at the end. Understand the basics of exactly what you are getting into, and what your status is. Ensuring you have a life distinct from his that is your safe haven can make being the other woman, if not a secure, permanent position, at least one that is a bit more tolerable.

CHAPTER 9

The Key to Saying No and Reclaiming Yourself
Has Anyone Here Seen My Life?

GILLIAN'S STORY

Every time Gillian looked at her calendar, she let out a sigh. She was one of those people who hit the ground running every day, and for her that meant literally. Five-thirty in the morning saw her out running to gear up for the day ahead. She needed this time to get her head clear and begin to focus on what she had to do throughout the long workday. And it was understood that it *would* be a long day; they all were. Gillian was a hardworking junior lawyer who never said no to the senior partner for whom she worked.

When Gillian was a thirty-year-old paralegal in the same firm, a tough no-nonsense lawyer named Carolyn told her she had a good legal mind and a solid grasp of corporate law. Why didn't she go to law school and become an attorney?

Gillian admired Carolyn, and more than that saw her as a strong female figure, a mentor. People said that Carolyn was "indispensable." Gillian wanted to have that said of her some day.

Gillian eagerly took the suggestion to heart, and following four years of night classes she had her J.D. and a large student loan. She became one of a pool of young lawyers at the same law firm where Carolyn worked. Soon she was assigned to a demanding man who was known for working the junior lawyers hard and getting rid of anyone who had a problem with working late or who said no to any job demands.

She went shopping for well-tailored business suits and expensive evening clothes even though it strained her budget because Carolyn had told her, "More deals are made at social functions than you can believe. You need to look stunning besides keeping your legal mind sharp and ready to close a deal before your competition does. This is the world of corporate law, Gillian, fascinating and cutthroat."

Her social life revolved around the firm's calendar. Working dinners, business deals brokered at parties, evenings spent socializing with clients consumed her nights and weekends. She had no time for a personal social life right now. She had to concentrate on her billable hours in the highly competitive legal industry. It was made crystal clear that anyone working less than a certain amount of hours could kiss his or her career at the firm good-bye.

Thirty-seven and unmarried, she always believed that she would have time to meet someone, settle down, and maybe have children. Gillian had hopes but no plans to get into the dating scene. But having been told by Carolyn on her first day at the firm that she should *never, ever say no* to anything you are asked to do here, and *always* get the job done no matter how late you have to work," Gillian never complained. The cleaning staff was careful not to disturb her. There were times she fell asleep at her desk and was awakened by the sound of the secretaries and paralegals coming in at 9:00 a.m. Then she'd go home for a couple of hours, shower, change clothes, and go back to work again.

She also heeded the strict warning that women have to be not just as good as their male counterparts but much, much better. She worked harder and longer hours than any male lawyer in the firm. Some of the men were married or in committed relationships, and Gillian saw that as a hindrance to getting ahead. There would be no roadblocks to success for her.

What's a Personal Life?

Gillian never spent more than a couple of days seeing her parents, brother, and sister-in-law over the holidays. She had so much to do at work that she felt she couldn't get away for a longer time. She was terrified of displeasing her bosses and not making partner someday.

Her brother told her she looked tired and her five-year-old nephew asked her why she was unhappy. "You know what would make you happy, Aunt Gillian? A vacation!"

Gillian just laughed at that. Vacation? Sure, when she could she would get away, but not right now; right now she owed her energy to her job. Hard work never killed anyone; it just made having a life outside of work difficult. Happy? Maybe someday when she didn't have to please an unpleasant boss. Besides, she was afraid to say no and be passed over for a promotion—or worse, lose her job. She still had that large student loan and a mortgage to pay.

When she was getting ready to leave after one brief holiday, her brother took her aside and said to her, "All you have is work. Don't you want more of a personal life,

Gilly?" She conceded that she did. But now wasn't the right time to think of a personal life.

It seemed the more Gillian did at the office, the more there was to do. Since she was known as someone who never said no to any project, no matter how big or time consuming, more work was thrown her way and more people needed her expertise. She was constantly in demand by other lawyers who knew that she would get them what they needed—and that her BlackBerry was on day and night.

Gillian began to model herself after Carolyn, who had helped her get her start in law. Gillian admired her mentor immensely. Carolyn had had a special couch put in her office for all-nighters when a case needed maximum attention. She longed to be as dedicated as Carolyn. Though she rarely saw Carolyn because they both had so much to do at the firm, Gillian still aspired to be just like her and worked harder than any other young lawyer to achieve her purpose.

Happiness is . . .
. . . knowing that life is ever-changing.
It pays to stop every so often and decide if you're going in the right direction. The journey called life does have a final destination, but before you reach it don't you think you should try to enjoy the trip?

Gillian became an attorney known for helping her firm get their clients the best corporate deals and for making sure that any legal problems that cropped up were swiftly resolved. She also had a well-earned reputation for making the partners happy and wealthy. All because she never said no.

Her personal life, however, was rather nonexistent. She rarely saw much of the very nice co-op she owned, spending most nights working past eleven. When she did entertain at home, it was mainly for business purposes, and she always had her eyes and ears open for new deals, new enterprises, new clients. The partners basically expected it of her.

As for dating, she had a few brief affairs with others in the profession and one very discreetly with a client, but they were physical acts of sexual release more than anything else. In fact when she found herself becoming seriously involved with one man who wanted to make their relationship more than it was, she abruptly broke it off. He still kept in touch with Gillian, but they rarely went out; when they did, all Gillian could talk about was her work. One night, walking her to a cab, he told her, "Gillian, you've got to have more in your life than just work. Any job that consumes you as much as this one does is stealing your life. Think seriously about what you want outside of the office."

But she didn't have much time to think. There were just so many hours in the day and she had to focus on what was important. There was never much time for anything else.

When she thought about it, Gillian knew she had to make some type of change in her life. It was all work, no play, no relaxation. Even her vacations were more or less working ones. But she had to please her boss to get ahead.

Indispensable Is Not Indestructible

Gillian had gone to her brother's house for the Thanksgiving holidays. As always, she had her laptop and her Black-Berry with her. Her niece and nephew were cute and tried to get Aunt Gillian to play games with them, but the firm had a client involved in a corporate takeover and her days were devoted to working out the details. In the midst of a houseful of guests, she stood out as the only one who hadn't left her work at the office for the holiday weekend.

While she was busy crunching numbers and finding the best way to help her boss's client achieve his goal, she received a call from a senior partner. This was nothing new; she was always being called for one thing or another. Gillian put the call on speakerphone while she continued working on her computer.

"Gillian? I'm calling to tell you that Carolyn had a stroke a few nights ago. No one knew. Her housekeeper only found her this morning. She died two hours ago."

The partner was obviously shaken as he went on to tell her that the hospital had no next of kin to call for "disposal of the remains." Did Gillian know about a will?

She couldn't believe what she was hearing! She had just seen Carolyn a few nights ago. It had been around eleven o'clock, and Carolyn had joked that she wouldn't be leaving until the sun came up, if at all. She'd wished Gillian a happy holiday and had gone back to working. Carolyn couldn't be gone. She was only fifty-eight!

But she *was* gone. Gillian cut short her holiday to get back to the office and unearth the will she knew Carolyn had had executed quite a few years ago.

In accordance with this will, the firm made the necessary final arrangements. Since Carolyn had no husband or children, her money and everything she had went to scholarships at her alma mater. Except for the people she had worked with over her long career, no one else attended the funeral.

At a restaurant where the members of the firm had gone after services for Carolyn, one senior partner took Gillian aside to speak privately. Gillian thought he was going to tell her he knew how hard this was for her since she and Carolyn had been so close. She was hardly prepared for what he had to say.

"Gillian, I'm giving you Carolyn's caseload. She was working on some very sensitive and important projects, and we have to go forward. I can't do it with all that's on my plate just now. The other partners and I know we can depend on you to get the work done."

Gillian was silent, and he took her silence for a yes. "You're indispensable, Gillian." *Just like Carolyn,* Gillian thought.

Satisfied, he went back to the group at the bar and left Gillian standing there alone and thinking about the word *indispensable.*

Two weeks later Carolyn's office was cleared out and given to another lawyer who changed everything to suit his tastes. It was almost as if Carolyn had never existed. Gone and not so indispensable after all.

In the weeks that followed, Gillian went about her days as usual. She was numb and sad but that didn't affect her work; in fact, it was work that kept her from thinking too much, and that was good. The nights at home were a different story. There she thought about being alone like Carolyn and having nobody at the end.

To finish one of Carolyn's projects, she had to get a folder from Carolyn's apartment. While she was there, Gillian saw the life that Carolyn had had. Evidence of Carolyn's profession was all over the apartment, but there was very little to reveal a personal life. There were pictures of Carolyn at business affairs and seminars, all of them work-related. She looked smart and sophisticated but not happy.

Gillian found the brief on the desk in the bedroom, and it was there that she saw a small framed picture of a smiling, happy, very young Carolyn. She was seated next to a good-looking man, and on her left ring finger was a small diamond ring. At first she didn't recognize the woman as Carolyn, so different was the woman in the picture from the polished, severe, professional image presented in the office. But this was indeed her mentor.

Gillian took the picture of Carolyn back to the office and showed the manager, who had been there for more than thirty years.

"Ah, yes, I remember her from back then. Very pretty young lady. She had been engaged and was so happy, but it didn't work out. She was a never-say-no type of woman, a workaholic. That type of attitude will kill any romance, and it did this one in. She could have had so much. What a wasted life!"

"Wasted? How could you say it was wasted?" asked Gillian. "She was a brilliant lawyer."

"Oh, wasted in a sense that all she had was work, she had nothing else. She was afraid to say no for fear of not getting ahead. A lot of women are like that. Don't let it happen to you. You're still young enough to make a change. Life needs equality."

Over the next year Gillian ran in the morning, did her work, came home exhausted, and said nothing, but there was that strange feeling inside that was making her feel dissatisfied and unfulfilled. Carolyn's dying alone in an empty apartment had affected her in a way she had not anticipated. She didn't want her own life to be considered a waste.

Gillian thought of little else now, even at work. She began taking a long hard look at her life and what her future might be. Staying late was no longer something she did without question. Most nights she was out the door before six. The senior partners didn't like it, but Gillian was numb to their disapproval. She did a tremendous amount of soul searching and called the one man with whom she could have had a serious relationship. He told her to weigh the pros and cons of what she had now against what she wanted.

Happiness is . . .

. . . knowing that you are meant to be happy. This is essential to achieving happiness now and in years to come. You were *born* happy; you were *programmed* to be unhappy. Decide what's important to you and balance your life.

"There's a whole lot more to living than work and being afraid to say no to your boss. You need to evaluate what's important. Teach yourself to say no."

That summer she requested a year's sabbatical to clear her head about what she needed to do with her life. As expected, the senior partners didn't take it well, warning her that being away from the office that long could be "professional suicide." But Gillian didn't care anymore. There had to be more to life than this building, these associates, and making money for others. Gillian had to reinvent herself.

She may have been "indispensable," but she wasn't an indestructible robot. Gillian never went back to the high-powered job. She eventually went into practice in a smaller firm where she made sure that her work life didn't become her whole life.

And she finally taught herself to say no.

•••

It is a sad comment on our society when a woman feels that to say no to a boss and his or her demands concerning work will lose her a promotion, a job, a career. The idea that women have to work harder than men in the same position to prove their "worthiness" may seem like a tired cliché left over from the 1980s, but unfortunately it is still true to some extent.

As Gillian found out, a healthy balance is crucial to a happy life. Work, though an important and very necessary part of existence, should not dominate your every waking moment. There is, and always should be, more to living.

COMBINING YOUR WORK AND PERSONAL LIVES: THE KEYS TO A HEALTHY BALANCED LIFE

You have every right to say no when you need to.
You may find it difficult the first time, but it becomes easier each time you say it. It may be wise not to say no *all* the time, since sometimes there are legitimate reasons for staying late or taking on more work. Be selective and know when to say *no*.

Stand up for yourself.

Have a meeting with your boss and tell him or her that while you understand that some late nights and extra work are inevitable, they shouldn't all fall on one person. Discuss the need to delegate minor aspects of your work to other employees who will answer to you. Don't be afraid to let your boss know what an excellent worker you are; this isn't vanity, it is fact. You have talents that are specific to your job, and you need to focus on those. If you're good at a particular job, you're good period. Let it be known.

Be wary of the word indispensable.

This is a word that has a subtle psychological tug. If your boss is telling you that he or she can't get along without you, that you are totally "indispensable to the business," be careful.

By believing that your boss can't get along without you, you are giving him or her license to take advantage of you. No one is indispensable or irreplaceable.

If you want to believe that you can't be replaced in your job, think of a favorite TV show where an actor walks away believing he cannot be replaced. Now think about how quickly he was replaced and how easily the show continued. Should you leave your job, you will be replaced almost immediately!

Know your legal rights.

There are laws against harassment. Being made to feel that you will be fired if you don't work crazy hours is a form of harassment. Check into the laws in the area where you work. However, keep this information discreet; don't make it part of the workplace gossip mill. Never tell a boss that he or she is breaking the law; the boss will find another way to fire you, usually by giving you a horrible work review. Be smart for your own self.

Seriously consider whether you want to stay in your job for the long run.

If your job is affecting your health or your relationships, it is time to decide how long you must remain in this unhappy work situation. It may not be in your best interests financially to just up and quit, but you can make the work situation tolerable by looking for another job while you are still employed. This is good psychologically because you feel empowered and in charge of your life. Give yourself a timetable and deadline for when you will be able to leave. Six months to two years with a little leeway for any unforeseen problems is a good rule of thumb.

You also need to be practical and have knowledge of your pension plan, any financial plans that can be rolled over into new ones, and any vacation days that, if not used, can be negotiated into pay. As upset as you are, you need to get advice on all these things in order to make plans for the future.

Reinvent yourself.

If you have an interest in another field, now is the time to make a career change. It may not even be a different field—perhaps you'd be happier in another department, for example, answerable to a different supervisor. Find out if your company has a tuition reimbursement plan or is willing to pay for you to take classes in something other than what you are doing at the present time. Doing work you actually enjoy is a big plus; planning for a new position can make your work life more bearable in the present.

One key thing to think about is that the grass is not always greener in a new job. All companies have overbearing bosses and aggravating work rules and expectations. Take the time to find out what suits you and what you need to make your abilities work for you. Saying no to what you don't want gives you power over your own existence whether in your personal life or on the job.

RECLAIMING YOUR PERSONAL LIFE 101: LESSONS LEARNED

The suggestion that in order for a woman to have a successful career she should say yes to any and all assignments is as wrong as it is sexist. Being born female does not mean you're born inferior. As a female executive once told me: "I refuse to be considered unworthy of a position simply because I don't urinate standing up! No one can tell me that fact has anything to do with intelligence and ability."

Strong words indeed, but a good honest evaluation of what self-worth should be.

If you feel inferior because you are female, it will pay you tremendous dividends in your life to ask yourself why you feel this way and what made you feel unworthy.

You don't have to see a therapist to find the answer. Look into yourself, then make it your business to change that learned negative attitude. You are worthy of all good things that come your way. Being a woman has less than nothing to do with being deserving.

Wanting to get ahead in your chosen field is normal. Whether it is law, education, nursing, or business, you have a need to make your mark. But there has to be a centering of your life, a balance that gives you both a professional life and a private one. Creating that balance is crucial to health. You owe yourself more than you owe an employer. There is no doubt that you need to be good at what you do, but you shouldn't allow it to become your entire life. You need a personal life as well a professional one to maintain a healthy equilibrium.

As for your job, it is also necessary for you to enjoy, to a certain extent, what it is you do every day. If you can manage to do that and maintain a separate personal area of your life, you will have created the best of both worlds.

Your work life has the possibility of surviving much more than your personal one. Why? Difficult though it may be at times, jobs can come and go. You may have many different ones during your lifetime. The work life will progress one way or another. Your personal life doesn't survive as well. Health, relationships, personal activities, friendships: All can be lost without some quality attention. You owe it to yourself to have a section of your life that is strictly personal where work will not interfere.

CHAPTER 10

The Key to Trying
Just Doing It

Fear is an emotion that has a dual purpose. Heeded in times of danger, it can literally save your life. That's the good part about fear. The bad part? Letting fear stop you from trying. Then fear blocks you from being alive in the way you really want to be. Fear of failing is a common thought. We are all afraid to fail at some level, but the people who succeed are the ones who overcome that fear. They don't see themselves as victims; instead, they see challenges.

A simple analogy is the small fear you may experience getting on a plane. You know all the things that *can* happen, but that doesn't stop you from boarding the plane. You overcome that fear because you have a desire to get to a specific destination and you have chosen to fly.

But there are some people who are afraid to get anywhere *near* a plane. They know that they will never get on it, don't see it as a viable choice of travel, and so don't even *attempt* to get on one. That fear stops them in their tracks. They are willing to put up with more inconvenient and lengthy modes of travel because of that fear. But there are other fears that paralyze as well.

CATE'S STORY

Cate's fear had nothing to do with tangible "real" fears like accidents or illness. Her fear was the fear of failure. She hoped that as the years passed, she might overcome this dread, but she never did and she never told anyone about it—or her dream.

By all accounts Cate was an intelligent woman who worked for the city library as the media director and had a good marriage. She was always busy at work or at home and always available to help others. There were many who were impressed with Cate. They didn't know that she had a secret. She kept up the pretense of being busy because she was afraid.

Being busy gave her an excuse not to do what she really wanted to do. Cate was a passionate photographer who had always harbored a dream of working for a magazine.

Her fear of failing had no real basis. Artistic efforts were encouraged in her family, and her parents bought her a professional-grade camera when she was only twelve years old. Her art teachers always told her she had a gift with images and was very creative. She enjoyed making portfolios. One of her teachers said that Cate should consider photography as a career.

In her senior year of high school, her dream of doing what she loved almost came true. A small local newspaper let the art department at the high school know they were looking for a student who would not only take pictures of town events, but also do a weekly fifteen-minute spot on a local news show. They asked the school to recommend several students. Cate's art teacher gave them Cate's name, and the newspaper called her to set up a date to come and meet the editor in chief. They also asked her to send sample pictures of her work to them a week before the interview. It was, her teacher said, a great opportunity.

Cate was excited and scared both at the same time. She wanted this so badly!

But Cate never sent in her work and she never went to meet the editor in chief. She was afraid that she wouldn't get the job. Her ideas and her talent were at once her gift and her secret agony. She couldn't bear to fail at something that was so close to her heart and meant so much to her. The teacher went with her second choice, a girl who was nowhere near as good a photographer as Cate but had a positive, can-do attitude. That girl got the position.

Cate would have loved being a student photographer. She cried over it a lot. But . . . she was terrified of failing.

The fear kept Cate from truly doing what she wanted.

Living so close to the city, Cate always knew when art competitions were held by the university. Twice a year they put on a photo and video contest, which was judged by renowned photographers whose own works frequently appeared in all the well-known magazines such as *Town & Country, Vanity Fair,* and *Harper's Bazaar.* Cate went so far as to fill out the submission entry form and meant to mail it. But somehow she always kept the envelope in her bedroom, agonizing over whether what she was doing was something she really wanted to do. She procrastinated so much that the deadline for submission came and went. Cate felt relieved that she hadn't had to make the decision to send it.

Cate had three boxes in her bedroom closet full of her portfolios. There was even a short series of seasonal photos she had made of the ocean. All of them were more than good and all of them were hidden away.

Living with Fear

Even with all the encouragement in the world from family and friends, Cate was afraid of failing to get her work published in a magazine or newspaper. She knew she had talent, but that fear kept her from doing anything about it. Sometimes she browsed magazine racks looking at photography in newspapers and magazines. In those moments she really thought she could send her work in to a few of them—but fear always stopped her. If her work was rejected, she wouldn't be able to handle it.

At home she worked in her darkroom or created designs on her computer for hours. She felt alive when she was doing what she loved. Maybe one day . . .

Time was not Cate's friend. She was letting too many things consume her life while she let her true passion go to waste. She kept herself incredibly busy so that she wouldn't have to face submitting her work and chance getting it rejected. Cate's frustration over not having the guts to try to get someone to look at her work began to weigh on her, and she started feeling depressed. She had talent, she knew she did, but what was it getting her? No one knew what she was capable of or what she really wanted to be.

Artistic people are by their very nature "different." Artists, musicians, and writers all have a burning need for a recognition of their work. Pursuing their art is as natural, and as necessary, to them as breathing.

Cate had no idea why she had a fear of failure, but it seemed to be an intrinsic part of her thinking. She ruefully understood that the reason she was so good at her library job was because there was absolutely no risk involved. She had nothing to prove, no danger of having her work rejected, and no one judging her on artistic merits. It was a bland job but a safe one. There was no chance of failure because there was no competition. She wasn't a competitor.

The buildup of frustration can take a heavy toll on an artistic person's emotions. This happened to Cate. She began feeling upset over the smallest things at work and at home. With her anger level so high, she snapped at others without a real reason. She was becoming increasingly angry with herself and her inability to take action for her career.

Cate found that she was becoming an emotional train wreck because of her fear. Her talent was burning inside her, and deep within her soul she knew that if she didn't do what she wanted to do, she would have wasted her life. The library wasn't a bad place to be, of course, but she longed to take a shot at her true passion.

Still, no matter how much she longed for it, she didn't act on it. She worked at her job while she daydreamed about doing something else.

Her husband saw her becoming withdrawn and angry and had no idea what was causing it. Finally one night when she was in the middle of developing pictures, he walked in and sat down just watching her work.

Glancing at the drying photos, he thought what she had done was really remarkable and said so. But when he asked her if the work was for a library display, Cate burst into tears.

All her pent-up emotion came through, and she found herself telling her husband how she hated the mundane work she did at the library. She wanted to quit her job. He had no idea what to say—but Cate did. The words just poured from her heart.

"I do not want another job, I don't want to quit and stay home and do nothing. And I don't want to be so busy for other people that I deliberately procrastinate about what is important to me. What I want," she said through tears, "is to send my photos and graphics to magazines. I want to be a professional media photographer. That is what I want, what I've always wanted. Maybe someday in the future . . ."

When he asked why she had never sent her portfolios to magazines, Cate answered sadly, "I am afraid of having my work rejected, I'm afraid of failing."

It was out in the open and her husband was relieved, if shocked. He'd had no idea Cate felt that way. She was always busy, always doing for others, and she had seemed to be okay with her life. Now that he thought of it, he could see signs that her nonstop schedule could be a way of coping with her fear.

At least now he knew what was wrong and, being a practical person, he felt that it could be dealt with. He asked Cate to show him her work, and they spent the next two hours going over her portfolios. Finally he looked at his wife and told her he truly felt she had real talent and that if becoming a media photographer was what she wanted, she should pursue it. He told her what he thought the problem was and why she didn't submit her photos. It was, he said, simple.

"You know what, Cate? It's not that you're afraid of failing. I think the real problem is that you have a fear of trying."

•••

Some women never try, not so much because they fear failure but because they have learned to expect failure.

ALEXA'S STORY

Alexa defined herself as a victim of fate. Everything that she tried seemed to go wrong. She blamed this on bad circumstances. She was to blame for nothing in her life because she took no personal responsibility for what happened. How could she be responsible? Her answer to everything was that she had had no choice; no matter what she did, it would have the same failing outcome. To say she was having a string of bad luck was an underestimation to her way of thinking.

So after a while she stopped trying altogether.

She met and dated the same type of man over and over again. Those relationships never worked out, and Alexa failed to see that she was simply repeating the same relationship mistakes with each man. But the failure of each relationship wasn't her fault; the wrong type of man was just attracted to her. She had no say in that matter. Again, it was fate.

Even when she dated a nice guy who was willing to work at a solid relationship, Alexa saw only another failure looming in her life. She was positive it wouldn't work out and it didn't, but that was due more to her negative misperceptions of relationships than anything else. Alexa brought the emotional baggage of past failed dating experiences to new and promising ones, ensuring that there'd be no success every time.

And friendships? Friendships were a torment for her, since she never knew why someone would want to be friends with her. What did she have to offer? Her friendships started out well but after a while they waned because Alexa didn't try to keep them going.

I *Always* Fail, Why Try?

It was the same with her career. She did take jobs that had *some* potential for advancement, but she only halfheartedly tried to get ahead. Her attitude was that of a chronic failure. Whenever she had an idea that she thought was good for a new project at work, she always second-guessed herself and never tried. The excuses for not trying were many: The people there didn't like her, her boss had it in for her, others might laugh at her. She hadn't been successful before and she wouldn't be now. Why risk it? Her negative victim mentality allowed opportunities at work to pass her by and kept her from succeeding in anything worthwhile.

Her expectation of failure prevented her from any real and much-needed change in her world. Still she daydreamed about happiness in the future when, by sheer accident, something good might happen.

Alexa was in a vicious cycle of life events. Her constant repeating of mistakes was similar to the story of a man who constantly bumps his knee on a piece of furniture whenever he walks into his living room. The man hopes each time he enters the room, it will be different. What he fails to understand is that the only way he will get a different result is by moving the furniture out of his way! In other words, for change to happen, for events to turn out differently, you have to make different choices than you've been making and move the negativity out of the way.

One day at a staff meeting, Alexa's new boss asked everyone present to present an original idea to increase sales. It was, he said, a great way to brainstorm and discuss any and all innovative options that anyone might have. When it was her turn to speak, Alexa was so scared that she hardly got her idea out of her mouth. No one commented on what she had said, the meeting went on, and she went back to her desk knowing that she was once again a victim of fate. She felt as if the others had thought her idea was dumb. To them she was sure she was an invisible person. Why, oh why, had she even tried? She was a failure!

But later her boss came to see her and told her that he thought her idea had potential; could she work on it and rephrase it for the next meeting?

He also asked her if she had any other suggestions for the project. Alexa was shocked and told him she didn't think that her idea was all that good.

He disagreed.

"It *is* good, Alexa. Just work on a few changes before you present to us."

He came to see her during the week, viewed her work, and made a few simple suggestions for change.

Two weeks later Alexa, barely able to speak because she was so nervous, presented her ideas to the staff. Not all were in agreement, but they were willing to discuss it, and Alexa felt a great relief. A colleague even said the plans were "not bad" and "possibly workable."

As they were walking out of the meeting, her boss told her he thought she had presented her idea very well. He had liked the way she gave specifics and detailed each step for new sales. When a surprised Alexa replied that she had never been successful in anything and just expected that she *never* would be, that she had always seemed to fail, her boss said thoughtfully, "Maybe that's because you've never really tried. Don't ever be afraid to try and retry an idea, and never be afraid to fail. Successful people are the ones who fail and still keep trying again and again. Keep up the good work. You've got a budding talent for creating solid plans."

Happiness isn't . . .

. . . fear of trying or simply not trying at all. If you don't try, you'll never know the joy of success. If you permit past failures to affect your present, you destroy any chance for a future that is different.

Alexa wasn't completely convinced that she had a talent for anything, and she still felt that something was bound to go wrong . . . but a tiny seed of possibility had been planted in her mind. Maybe, just maybe, she should try to see what she could do.

•••

Some women are so sure they will fail at something that they never try at all. Some psychiatrists say that being afraid to try can also mean you have a victim mentality. Why bother? Why even think about it? Nothing ever works out the way you want it to no matter what you do. You feel as if success won't happen simply because you are a victim of fate and other people. You can only hope that your luck will change in the future. You daydream what life will be like when and if fate changes. Unfortunately you are not a doer who is willing to assist fate and make changes allowing it to happen.

BELIEVE IN YOUR UNIQUE ABILITIES TO SUCCEED: THE KEYS TO OVERCOMING THE FEAR OF FAILURE

The keys you need are the ones that help you understand why you fear the worst. The first key is . . .

Being afraid to fail is normal, but don't be afraid to try. There is one thing worse than failure, and that is the fear of trying. Cate's husband was right: She had a fear of even attempting her dream career. Pointing out the true reason Cate was unhappy gave her a starting point to change her perspective and her life. Cate constantly said to herself that someday she might get up the courage to submit her portfolios, but that sounded hollow even to her. She knew she never would. She just had to do it!

Alexa felt that she had no choice but to be a victim of fate. She feared to try because she had convinced herself that no matter what she did, it wouldn't work out right. Her past mistakes made her create a mind-set that nothing good would ever come her way unless it was by accident. Her boss made the right comment to her when he said she had never really tried.

Don't wait for the right moment to do something. If you do, you might be waiting the rest of your life. You need to overcome your procrastination and take the first step no matter how frightened you may be.

Talented people are afraid to fail, too.
People do not fail in life because of lack of skill. They fail because they do not try. You need to know that while failure may be a negative word, the simple explanation is entirely different. Failure means that the outcome of something you attempted was not the one you wanted or anticipated. If you fail, you shouldn't give up. The lesson is that what you tried didn't work, so retry it or try it in a different way.

Consider the personal cost of wasting your potential.
Every time you give in to the fear of trying, you have missed an opportunity. Each one you miss costs you in time and self-esteem. You are defeating your purpose in life. Your talent will lie dormant each time you allow fear to prevent you from achieving your desired goal. Failing is certainly not fun. Who wants to fail? But if you choose not to take some risks, you are giving up a powerful path to strong living. Fear of trying becomes a habit that is difficult to live with but even harder to break.

Having a victim mentality stops you from having choices.

Design a **What if I do fail scenario** . . . *then decide your course of action.*
Knowing that you might actually fail at something shouldn't keep you from trying—but you do need a backup plan. How will you handle failure? What can you do to make failing have as little an impact on your dreams as possible? The most positive part of your plan should be that you will try again immediately.

You cannot give up or you will fall into the same pattern of not trying as before.

The second part is to understand that rejection is not personal, it is not you; everything is subjective and what one person doesn't like, someone else will. I once sent a humor story about a married couple to an editor. He rejected it but did give me a reason for his decision. He was going through a divorce and a story about a married couple, humorous or not, just didn't sit well with him at that moment. I tried another editor at a different magazine and the same exact story was accepted. It had nothing to do with my writing; it had to do with the individual interpretation of it.

Know your own potential and capabilities.
You've got to blow your own horn or you'll never get heard!

You know your own talent but if you're the only one who knows how good you are, exactly how are you benefiting from it? The best chef in the world is not the best if no one tastes her cooking, a Mozart can remain unknown unless someone hears his music, and the most beautiful flower in the world may actually be growing in a desert oasis but no one will ever know of it unless it is brought to everyone's attention. No one knows you better than you know yourself. Family and friends may *think* they know you, but all they are seeing is what you present to them, what you want them to see. Even a person living with you, sleeping with you in the same bed, does not know the real you. Your dreams, your fears, your abilities are inside you.

OVERCOMING FEAR OF FAILURE 101: LESSONS LEARNED

If you are interested in pursuing a dream, you have to be prepared for some type of failure. That shouldn't stop you from trying. It is a sad woman who spends years afraid to try and realizes that the only thing keeping her from what she wanted was her own fears.

Dreams are meant to be pursued. Any missed opportunity is a missed chance for the realization of your dream. It would be nice if everything we wanted came to us without any risk or work, but that isn't going to happen. You have to be the one to pursue what will give you satisfaction and contentment.

There are many stories of people who have tried, failed, and tried again. What do they have that you don't? Nothing at all, except tenacity and a determination that at some point, they will succeed. To them, the idea of never knowing if they will succeed is infinitely worse than trying and failing. You don't want to be a woman who says, "If only I had . . ." never knowing for sure if you would have succeeded.

Am I saying that you should be content with what you have now? Yes, but . . .

Let's be realistic. Constantly dreaming about something will not get you what you want. It takes planning and effort. However, while you're planning for your future, don't miss out on the life you have now. Don't be afraid to be happy because you somehow feel that, if you are happy, you'll never put the effort into making changes.

The fear of trying or not trying at all over and over again sends you a clear message that says, I'm not worthy of getting what I want. Don't let that be your standard attitude. Try and try again. Fail and try, but always keep on trying. Any dream is worth a chance. You are worthy of seeing your dream realized.

CHAPTER 11

⚷ The Key to Learning That Perfection *Isn't* Happiness
The "Perfect" Woman Needs a Break!

Some women make everything look easy. They always look great, run errands with ease, balance family and work seamlessly, throw fantastic parties, have decorator homes, and never miss a beat in being fashionable *and* in the know. (You may even be striving to become one.) But while you admire them, you also have a certain dislike for them.

Why aren't *I* perfect, too? What's wrong with *me*?

Actually there's nothing wrong with imperfect you. What you don't know is that the perfect woman runs her perfect life at great expense. The expense isn't monetary; it is a personal cost that the woman herself pays in stress. She pays with both her physical and emotional health, and the cost gets higher as the years go on.

TINA'S STORY

Tina was the perfect woman; at least everyone thought she was. She was an excellent mother, wife, friend, and employee. She always looked as if she stepped out of a fashion magazine, and her home looked as if it should be in the pages of a book on interior design.

Want a fabulous party? Go to Tina's house. Need help with something, anything at all? Call Tina. Someone called in sick at work? Tina is more than willing to help out. Tina was the wife who made herself gorgeous and sexy for her husband, lucky guy! The mother whom all the teachers liked, which was great for her kids, the friend who could help you plan everything from a World Series barbecue to a bridal dinner, and the co-worker who made her area of the workplace run efficiently while still having time to plan all the office parties. She had it all, did it all well, *was* perfect, and happy. Or so it seemed.

In reality Tina was a ticking time bomb created by all her perfection, and she certainly wasn't happy. The perfect life was exacting a severe toll on her all-too-human self. She smoked way too much, suffered from insomnia and panic attacks, and was on medication for hypertension. Yet she ably maintained the facade of a woman who had it all under control and gave the illusion that there was absolutely no flaw permitted in her world.

Tina came from a long line of perfect women. In her quest for perfection, she was following her mother and grandmother, women who made perfection *seem* not only easy but normal. They never allowed themselves to be seen as vulnerable or unable to carry out all the major details of running a perfect life. Tina was just upholding a female family tradition of living a certain way, the only way.

She didn't expect to be happy; she couldn't. While others saw her life as perfect, Tina saw it as something that could always stand to be improved. There was always some area of her home, her personal appearance, or her marriage that she could and should make better. It was exhausting always anticipating what changes she could make to have everything the very best it could be. And she was never alone for any much-needed downtime.

Tina had once asked her grandmother if *she* was happy with her life. Her grandmother's response was, "Happiness depends on perfection. Life without perfection, Tina, is a life half lived. And you are lucky that *your* generation can have it all."

With an answer like that, no wonder Tina felt that nothing was ever perfect enough and she had to keep on striving for more simply to uphold the "family honor"! If she didn't have perfection, how the hell could she ever hope to be happy?

Happiness is . . .

. . . knowing that you aren't going to be perfect in everything and that you don't need to be. Be yourself. Know your limits; don't equate happiness or a well-lived life with perfection and having it all.

So everything Tina did had to be just right, and if it wasn't she could blame no one but herself. Meals at her house weren't just meals, they were nutritious and gourmet. And speaking of her house, it was as well maintained as a museum; nothing was ever out of place. She was never late for anything and always made a beautiful appearance. Her own family never saw her without makeup. Smart, witty, charming, perfect Tina.

Tina's husband benefited from her perfection and had no reason to question if she was happy, nor did her children. Everyone, her family, close friends, and co-workers, only saw what she wanted them to see—a woman who was able to do it all well.

If anyone envied Tina it was because they didn't know the real person inside her. That person, the imperfect Tina, was a scared little girl who had to have absolute control over every aspect of her life. If she didn't, her world would fall apart. She longed for happiness and dreamed about what she would do when she had the time to be herself.

The Tina everyone knew in her perfect world had a conflict with the Tina she really wanted to be.

Women Who Have a Bad Hair Day Are Blessed

No one suspected this, but Tina envied her friends who envied her! She would have loved to have a bad hair day like everyone else. It would be wonderful to be outside in old sweats instead of wearing designer "lounge wear." Ordering pizza for dinner, being late to work, not always having to put on a show that everything was okay when it wasn't, that was what Tina wanted. At least she wanted to try it once in a while. It seemed much easier!

But that wasn't her life, and she didn't know any other way to live. She had to keep on being the perfect woman or a very believable semblance of one. Tina became the victim of her own perfection.

Tina's house of perfect cards came tumbling down when her panic attacks started becoming more severe. For no reason that she could understand, the attacks were occurring at very inappropriate times. She might be in the middle of dinner at a restaurant and her hands would suddenly begin to shake. In a room full of people in her own home, she would break out in a cold sweat with a feeling that she was trapped.

Finally Tina found herself doing something she had never done before: losing her temper over the smallest things and finding that she felt an enormous pressure to "get everything done." Perfect women shouldn't feel that way, should they? But she couldn't help it.

The day she got into an argument over having to wait in a long line at a home decorating store, burst into tears, and couldn't stop crying was the beginning of her breakdown and, in a strange way, her salvation. She simply couldn't do everything perfectly anymore.

When Tina eventually had a breakdown and was unable to do anything at all, her grandmother delicately called it an "exhaustive collapse." In the midst of a crisis, even something as serious as an emotional breakdown had to be explained in perfect words. Saying exhaustive collapse sounds so much better than "Tina finally snapped!"

Rather funny but sad comment considering the fact that Tina was lying in bed in borrowed baggy sweats, unable to go to work, and finally having her bad hair day. But it was no joke, and polite language couldn't make the problem sound any nicer. Tina had an emotional breakdown and that was a plain fact no matter how ugly the words sounded.

Tina was depressed and miserable. She felt that she was letting everybody down, especially the women in her family who had made the perfect life seem so easy and so necessary.

What was wrong with *her?* Why couldn't she simply continue keeping up a facade of perfection? Where would she find her happiness if she didn't have her perfection?

Wandering around her perfect house in her new imperfect state, she didn't know what she could do to get back to being the woman she was used to being. She needed a new strategy for life.

●●●

You can't and shouldn't control everything. Life is messy; you can't control it. Isn't it a relief to know that some things are out of your direct control? You can't control the weather or unexpected delays no matter how good your plans are. No one should try to control everything. There are bound to be upsets and imperfections. Even a so-called perfect diamond has a tiny flaw in it somewhere. That is nature and that is life.

THE MYTH OF PERFECTION: THE KEYS TO "PERFECTION" REALITY

Jill of all trades, mistress of none.
You cannot do it all and do all of it well. When an executive of a high-powered corporation was asked if she thought the modern woman of the twenty-first century could have it all, and all at once, she replied, "Oh, no. *Something* has to give. You can't be good at everything all the time. You need to focus on one area where you excel and even then, be prepared for less than perfect. Having it all is a Madison Avenue myth."

She is right: Your job, your creativity, your family, your own peace of mind will suffer if you try to do it all. The commercials, the magazine ads all contribute to the myth of what we should have. You can bet good money that the models in the media don't really have it all; it is all a grand illusion. By expecting to have it all and all at once, you can end up having *nothing* at all.

What you *can* have are times where you are happily successful in one area and doing okay in another. A good example of this is a career surge when you have just about everything running smoothly. Your personal life, while still good, might be taking a backseat for a while. That vacation you want or a move to a new place will have to just wait for a bit. Turnabout is bound to come when your career takes a smaller role in your life while your personal goals become more prominent. You get to take that trip to Bermuda; the move to the house or apartment you wanted does occur. Balance and harmony in all areas of your life definitely at the same time—but not perfection.

Follow your own rules for your own life.

Simple statement: My game, my rules. Your life is the game and your choices in how you live it are the rules. You can bend the rules a little bit for different situations, but you shouldn't bend them so much that they break. You can also change the rules as you go along, but keep in mind that the rules you create are there to benefit your well-being; don't change them so much they become unrecognizable. Remove the self-imposed burden that is the need to be the perfect woman. Constantly trying to be perfect means never achieving satisfaction in any area of your life. See yourself in reality. You're not superwoman, and the great thing is you don't need to be. Doing what you can with what you have is perfection enough.

Have a fortress of solitude.

You need downtime! It worked for the Man of Steel, it can work for you, too. It can be a place as simple as a corner of a room where you daydream or listen to music or read undisturbed. As nice as it would be, you don't need to build a large getaway to have time for yourself. You just need an unbreakable rule that thirty to sixty minutes out of a day belong to you alone. That's not a lot to give to yourself, but it gives you uninterrupted time to be "the Woman of Steel" in her own environment. The world will function quite well without your constant vigilance, and guess what? . . . so will you.

Remember, you're not perfect—but you're perfectly normal.

Have you ever thought that you needed a personal assistant to help you with all the many demands of your chaotic life? You are one person yet you are called upon to do so many things. You've become a master multitasker and you need time off. How nice it would be to have someone who could help you on a daily basis!

But having a personal assistant is not something most of us can afford. So you continue to struggle with all you have to do and always feel that you don't measure up to perfection because there is something lacking in you. However . . .

There is nothing lacking in you. The perfection you so prize can never be real.

Take a break and do nothing.
How nice would it be to simply not be available? To take a much-needed break from everyone and everything that demands your attention?

Too many times you rush from one task to another and never allow yourself to just do nothing. Heaven forbid you're idle! But not being available is an "action" that allows you to stop and take a breather—and that is what you need. While you're idle, stop thinking of what you need to do next on that unending list that constantly needs your attention. It can wait.

PERFECT YOU VERSUS IMPERFECT YOU 101: LESSONS LEARNED

What does trying to be perfect really get you? It doesn't get you a perfect life, far from it. What it *does* get you is tremendous stress, lack of sleep, constant vigilance about everything you need to do, no "me" time, possible health problems, and a hectic lifestyle that you will be unable to maintain for very long. You need to let go of the idea that you need to be perfect in all that you are and do.

You don't have to let go of everything in your busy day, but prioritize what is really important to you in your life. Choose a few areas where your perfection and expertise will do some good. Make a list of what you really *need* and *want* to do. Be completely honest with yourself about *why* you need to be perfect. Can you be even slightly off?

Think of the 1970s original movie *The Stepford Wives,* based on the 1972 book of the same name by author Ira Levin. Surreal, scary, and thought provoking all at the same time. Women were turned into perfect, smiling robotic images of themselves just so they were able to make life wonderfully happy for everyone in their families and communities. Did making others happy and having everything be perfect finally make *them* happy? No! Why? They were robots!

The term *stepford* has become part of our vocabulary thanks to that movie. It's used as an adjective to describe a person as "eerily and unnaturally perfect, robotic." But the perfect woman you may admire cannot exactly be described as "eerily and unnaturally perfect" because of one important detail: Unlike the "robo-woman" in the movie, the real perfect woman has emotions and a definite breaking point.

Perfection may be an ideal that is pushed on us by the media—where everyone and everything looks fantastic *all* the time—but it is an impossible goal and one you shouldn't even try to achieve. A life that has no messes in it is an impossibility.

The woman who tries to have every single thing in her life run smoothly on well-greased wheels is the woman most likely to break down emotionally and eventually physically. The more she does, the more she will do, because perfection becomes an obsession. To reduce stress, many women begin self-medicating either with prescription drugs or alcohol. They are not happy because they are always seeking the next level of perfection. They can't let anyone down even though they are certainly letting themselves down. It is an exhausting, never-ending quest.

So perfection is actually a hindrance to your search for a happy life. You live your days forever anticipating and never getting to enjoy what you've already done and what you have in your life now. Perfection is never satisfied. There's always more to do.

What's the worst that can happen if you're not perfect? Nothing! You'll survive and you'll be healthier, too. Try being a little imperfect, it's so good for you. By not trying to be perfect in all ways to all people, you are doing yourself a huge favor. A little messiness in your life is actually good for you. You *are* human, you *will* make mistakes, you will *not* get everything done, and you will *survive* quite nicely. That's reality, and that's good.

CHAPTER 12

⚷ The Key to Living Life Fully
Preparing for and Creating Your Own Opportunities

One way that you can sabotage your chances for happiness is in the area of opportunities. Either you are not fully prepared to take advantage of an opportunity that comes your way, or you don't take the initiative and create an opportunity of your own if one doesn't exist.

We all want to have that chance, to get that lucky break, to have the occasion for something special. It can be landing a great job, meeting the right person, making a good connection, getting that fantastic place to live, or finally achieving a dream. It's out there, you know it is; all you have to do is wait.

Actually you have to do much more than just want it and wait for it. Opportunity doesn't come to those who sit back and wait. Not at all. What you may not realize is that opportunity needs a little help to find its way to you and knock on your door.

You help yourself by carefully preparing to get what you want. An example of this is saving money for a new car. You have a generalized idea of what you want in a car but haven't found the right one yet. However, the fact is that you're *preparing* to get it by saving money toward a down payment. You are also keeping your eyes open for just the right car. That is preparing for opportunity. When it comes, you will be ready.

Creating opportunity is a bit different. Perhaps you've been looking for a new career. You don't see anything that you really want in the field you've chosen, but you have great ideas that need to be expressed. So instead of going from one interview to another hoping to find the ideal position, you decide to start your own small business where you can have creative control. Many successful people in business and the arts have made their own opportunities when they were dissatisfied with what was available to them elsewhere. You can, too. By doing this you create your own opportunity.

Too many times you allow yourself to be discouraged. You become tired of hoping, or not getting that chance, or you think opportunity will never come to you. You stop making yourself ready for a break and don't prepare for opportunity's knock on the door. Because you are unaware of your own potential and abilities, you also never think to create your own chances.

Being unprepared for a break is a guaranteed way to make sure that knock on the door will go completely unanswered. You have made absolutely certain that you are not ready to take advantage of the chance for which you have been waiting. Opportunity can be fickle. Sometimes it will only knock once. If you're not ready, it may be lost forever.

There are too many stories about not being prepared for "that lucky break." A missed chance is forever a reminder that you let something you wanted slip away. Can it be recaptured? Sometimes. Emma was lucky to have a second chance for her lucky break. All she needed was preparation.

EMMA'S STORY

Emma, an aspiring ballet dancer, remembers that not being prepared for opportunity cost her dearly in her profession. It almost made her miss the chance for a starring role that could make her career.

Ballet was her passion. She had been dancing since her childhood and was determined to make it her life's work. In her life as a dancer, her classes and practice sessions took more than eight hours every day, but that was perfectly fine with her. Practice did make perfect, and she felt completely prepared for any opportunities. She was waiting for her big break. It was coming; she could feel it. For a long while she was enthusiastic and eager.

But several years of auditioning for any and all roles, only to be assigned minor ones—or worse, placed in the chorus line time and again—took its toll on her attitude. She stopped preparing herself for her big break. Why put yourself through all the work if you're not going to get what you want? With that reasoning, she downsized her day-to-day routine.

Instead of the daily rigor of intense practice, Emma cut her sessions to two times a week. She became lethargic about dancing and didn't, as she says, "dance with my whole body and spirit." Auditioning for roles, she found herself out of step and slightly off in all her routines. Because she was not as good as she could be or totally prepared for *any* dance roles, she didn't get even the small parts any longer. It had a depressing effect on her attitude and her career. Emma was not truly living; she was existing in her life.

She went on this way for about a year, which is a long time in a dancer's life. You are only as good as your last performance. Busy choreographers and dance company heads who hire dancers base many of their decisions on whom they have seen recently and what type of reviews the dancers have received from critics. If you cannot point to a recent excellent review of a performance or have nothing striking to show in your repertoire, your chances of getting a role are very limited.

Unprepared Means Being Out of Step with Your Dream

Emma continued going on auditions but was becoming more and more discouraged. She began making excuses not to go to her practice sessions. Of course when she was at her lowest point, an opportunity for a coveted lead role opened up in a major dance company. She had wanted this role ever since she began dancing. Emma wanted to be one of the prime candidates for it and managed through a friend to be allowed into a private pre-audition. But when her turn to dance came, her performance was mediocre at best.

She knew she would be immediately cut from consideration for the role and walked off the stage with tears in her eyes. The ballet director, who had seen her dance a few years before and knew what she was capable of, asked her what had happened to her perfect timing and grace.

"You used to be wonderful. What happened to you?"

Emma told him the whole story about always being frustrated at not getting roles when she had practiced so much for each one. She had stopped preparing for opportunity because she was tired of "waiting for my chance."

The director told her that she would have been brilliant in the role. He also told her that they would be holding open auditions next month. If she was willing to make her practice sessions a priority, she could try again. It was possible that she'd get a role; you never knew.

Emma thanked him and said she was willing to take another chance.

Then she did something she had never done: Emma begged him to hold off selecting the lead dancer until he could see her new audition. Luckily for her, this director—who enjoyed seeing her dance and felt she lit up the stage even in the small roles she had been assigned in the past—agreed.

A month later, after many hours of preparation and practice, she danced brilliantly and got the leading role.

"After that experience, I made sure that, no matter what, no matter how many times I was disappointed or frustrated in my career, I would always be prepared for the possibility of opportunity," she said. "Not being prepared is the same as not being serious about what is important to me. *Living* my life is the only way for me to be happy. Dancing well *is* living well for me."

•••

Opportunity may not always present itself to you. Sometimes you have to make that knock on the door happen. You may need to create your own opportunities to fulfill your life.

HEATHER'S STORY

Heather firmly believed opportunity came when you least expected it. She was right about that. Where she was wrong in that belief was in thinking that fortune would come without preparation or creative help of any kind on her part.

She dreamed about leaving her job as an administrative assistant.

Heather was tired of the boredom of her workdays and had lost interest in the job she'd had for better than ten years. She didn't know exactly what she wanted; all she knew was that she was eager for a change. Heather felt that all she had to do was wait for the right opportunity for something better to come along. It would come in time, and then she'd be happy in a new career.

Heather had various talents and interests, any one of which she could have begun to sharpen in her quest for a new job. She was good at arranging travel plans for her boss, which would have been an ideal segue into a career in the travel industry. She could even get a job working as the business travel coordinator for another company. Those positions had crossed her mind, but she hadn't acted on them.

Her ability as a speaker was an asset that she could have turned into a marketing career, but she hadn't taken the time to explore that idea even though she'd thought about it. And she also had a knack for teaching complicated corporate issues to new employees, which could lead to a job in public or corporate education.

She mulled over the ideas in her head from time to time but did nothing to make a change or seek a way for a new job. Heather stayed where she was and kept assuming a change of career would automatically and unexpectedly come her way soon.

Meanwhile she was stagnating in her professional life instead of living it. Her thoughts about *changing* her career did nothing to *make* it happen. Whenever she heard about people who had successfully changed careers or begun a new phase in their lives, she felt it was because opportunity had come knocking on their doors. She never thought that anyone had actually *prepared* to make changes or *created* their own lucky breaks. It was simply a matter of having had the unexpected right opportunity.

Who's Lazy?!

Heather suffered from "comfortable laziness," but she would have been shocked to hear anyone say that. She did her job and did it well, bored or not. In her personal life, she certainly wasn't lazy. Everything that had to get done *did* get done. But the things she was doing required no initiative or new ideas. Her job and her life had a sameness that was comfortable for her. She never had to do anything differently. Because of this she did nothing to prepare herself for the possibility of something new.

Had Heather looked for a new position, she would have seen many opportunities for a woman with her abilities. She could have made some significant efforts to be ready for opportunity's knock or actively sought to make her own lucky break. She chose to do neither.

No Plans, No Change, No Satisfaction

Heather went on this way for quite a while, waiting for that "knock on the door" but making no plans for when it did come. With this attitude she was destined to always be waiting and never making necessary changes. If opportunity did present itself in the form of a new career, she would not be ready to make the move no matter how much she wanted it. *Wanting* is not the same as *doing*. If she wasn't ready to make her own chance for a career change, she was saying she was content with just drifting through life. Either way, she wasn't getting anywhere with her mind-set.

Preparing for opportunity or even creating your own opportunity coupled with determination are key to any success in life. Luck is actually the smallest part of opportunity.

OLYMPIC GOLD IS NOT WON UNLESS YOU ARE PREPARED: THE KEYS FOR CREATING AND PREPARING FOR OPPORTUNITIES

Every Olympic hopeful knows three things:

One: You have *less* of a chance of winning the gold if you give a *less*-than-stellar performance.

Two: To give the best performance you can, you need to put in hard work and be prepared.

Three: Opportunity comes when luck and preparation meet.

Be in the right place at the right time.
You've heard of someone being in the right place at the right time? You might believe that that person was just lucky. However, luck has less to do with it than you realize. Being in the right place at the right time takes plenty of good planning and foresight. A person with that kind of luck has prepared for or personally created both the place and the time. Fortune does well with good planning. This helps you to live life fully.

Most events don't just happen in life without a considerable amount of preparation. This is especially true if the event is something you've been hoping for. Hope doesn't help you get it. You need to be able to be ready for an opportunity. While not meaning to sound like a Girl Scout, the best advice still is to be prepared for life.

Be available for opportunity.
Too many times you feel hopeless that your dream will ever be realized and you stop preparing yourself for that golden opportunity. That is one of the biggest mistakes you can make. You never know where or when opportunity will come. It arrives in its own sweet time and never when you expect. Being ready to accept and follow your dream to wherever it takes you not only makes perfect sense, but is necessary to the survival of your dream.

Opportunity comes on time whether you are ready or not. A simple analogy is taking a train to a destination for an important appointment. If the train will be leaving the station at 8:00 a.m. sharp, you need to plan to leave your home at a specific time in order to be at the station for that train. It will arrive regardless of whether you are there or not. If you haven't prepared to be at the station on time, you will miss the opportunity to take that train. Another train will come along eventually, but it won't be the same.

Create your own opportunity.

How often have you felt that life had passed you by while others seem to get opportunity after wonderful opportunity? Now ask yourself what those lucky people do that you aren't doing. What changes do they make to allow themselves to be ready? It is simple. They are *committed to creating* their own chances for success. They leave nothing to chance.

My own career is a small example. When I was a high school teacher, I never let go of my true goal of becoming a writer. I worked toward getting my name known in the writing community by sending out hundreds of articles and stories via e-mail and by regular mail. Even though I knew that making a decent living in writing was chancy at best, that for every best-selling author like Dan Brown or Candace Bushnell, there were thousands of struggling hopefuls like me; even though for every acceptance letter I received there were ten rejecting my work, I kept at it. I was preparing myself for that proverbial knock on the door from opportunity and eventually it did come.

Make a commitment to be fully aware of what possibilities await you and how best to meet the challenges of making changes for what you want. You will avoid missing out on what is available to you by making necessary preparations or creating your own luck. You won't stumble or hesitate on your way to the door to answer opportunity's knock. You'll be more than ready.

Look at the whole picture.

Too often you allow yourself to see your daily life only peripherally. You put on blinders so that you focus only on what you need to do every day. Anything outside that is a distraction. You neglect to see what you can do and can have if you make the right plans.

To be ready and willing for life's chances or to invent your own break is making a serious promise to yourself that you are ready for a new and exciting part of your life.

Whether you prepare for opportunity or you decide to create your own, you are completely alive. That is what is meant by the saying, *The happiness of life is in living it fully.* If you do not prepare for chances that you want or create new possibilities, you are saying that you are content to live in limbo.

You also need to know that new opportunities will come at different periods of your life. Your abilities and needs change as you go through life. What you need and want at twenty-five isn't the same as what you need and want at fifty. Be alert to what is available at all phases of your life.

The opportunity is there; you just have to find it.

What opportunity are you waiting for? How do you intend to prepare for the possibility of it arriving? Do you want to act in theater, own a horse, begin a business, travel the world, learn to scuba, take ballet lessons, buy a Jaguar, paint in watercolor, sing opera, run a marathon, write a book, ice skate, join a rock band, learn a language, go back to school, become an archaeologist, run for office? These are only some of the things women have told me they had wanted to do.

Opportunity is best used when you have a clear knowledge of what you really want to do. Then you can focus on finding the right opportunities that best fit your needs. That's being smart, being prepared, and being ready to reap all rewards.

OPPORTUNITIES 101: LESSONS LEARNED

Who does nothing need hope for nothing.
Friedrich von Schiller

Action is the primary requisite of making changes. Thinking, planning, creating, and preparing are all part of action. It may seem as if these ideas are simple no-brainers. You should know them. But more often than not, you don't realize until it is almost too late that most of life doesn't *just happen.* It would be great if your life was programmed right from birth to give you everything you will ever need or desire at exactly the right time and place. That won't happen. Sometimes you need to design the program that is best suited to you as an individual. The way to do that is by careful evaluation of what it is you want, what you will need to get it, and how you intend to get there. Dreams? Great! Planning or creating? Better!

Being available for the possibility of opportunity can give you what you want. Be open for any and all changes. You may not ever act on Broadway, but you may be a star in *regional* theater. You might not ever dance the lead in *Swan Lake,* but you will find pleasure and satisfaction in taking dance classes. You may not circumnavigate the globe, but you can pick one country you truly wish to visit and explore it.

Realize that the reality for change is good. Begin a business? Why not? Learn about starting a small business and see where it takes you. Be the CEO of your own world! And why not buy or lease your dream car? If that's not possible, at least go take a test drive! *What* are you *waiting* for? The options and opportunities for your dreams are endless. They can become reality if you prepare for them or are willing to create your own.

CHAPTER 13

♀ Happiness Insights
The Answers

Remember the quiz you took? Have your ideas about happiness changed after reading the stories and keys? Are you thinking of making some life changes that will enable you to live happily and realistically? That's great! Let's review the questions and see what keys can help you make some needed changes. Remember, there are no wrong answers, just honest ones. Everything in your life can change for the better. Ready? Here we go!

THE KEYS TO REALISTIC HAPPINESS AND LIFE CHANGES

QUESTION 1.
How do you wake up in the morning? Do you dread the day ahead every day?
Wake up with anticipation.

While no one wakes up in a good mood on a daily basis, you should not dread opening your eyes and getting out of bed every day, either. Try this simple test for a week. Before you go to bed, write down one pleasurable thing you are going to do the next day. Make it something that you look forward to such as having a good cup of coffee made just the way you like it or going to a park for a short walk. Anticipation of a pleasure is a good motivator for waking up. Every day you open windows that affect your life.

Open windows give views that can alter a mood. How would you feel if you opened a window only to look out at a dark, barren landscape day after day? It would certainly have a negative impact on your feelings, wouldn't it? You'd feel like going back to bed and hiding; you certainly wouldn't want to leave the house!

But if you saw a beautiful summer garden through a window each morning, you would anticipate going out into the glorious day. Staying indoors would not be an option.

If you dread the day ahead of you and are always wishing the hours away, the view you have is negative and you will feel miserable all day. However, if you have even a small feeling of excitement about what your day will bring, you will welcome every single minute.

QUESTION 2.
Are you always last on your to-do list?
Put yourself first.

What is a list for? To prioritize. You put the important things at the top of the list. If you think that you have to help everyone else before you can get around to helping yourself, you are making a huge mistake. It's been said before but this bears repeating: When we board a plane for takeoff, we are told that if there is an emergency, we should put our own oxygen mask on first before assisting others. In other words, take care of yourself first; that will put you in a much better position to help someone else.

If you needed help, who would better serve your needs: a person who is tired, overwhelmed, and hasn't taken care of herself? Or the woman who cares for herself, is mentally alert, and enjoys good physical health? Obviously you would choose the latter, no question. That person exudes strength, success, and confidence in all ways. Prioritizing you first helps you become that person.

QUESTION 3.
How would you *like* to direct your energy and time to fulfill your life?

Be positive and let your energy work for you.
Negativity is more powerful than being positive because it is easier to sustain. There's not a whole lot you have to do to keep it going. On the other hand, to be able to see life in a positive way requires effort.

You have to turn any distressing situation into a manageable one that can have a decent outcome. That takes work, but it's worth it. Imagine what you could accomplish with your life if you put your energy and time into what you really wanted to do! This life is your life, not your parents', not your significant other's, not your children's, not your boss's, and certainly not that negative idiot in your head whose voice keeps telling you that "you can't be happy until . . ." That voice has got to go! Silence your inner critic and begin to use your time and energy on improving your life.

QUESTION 4.
Who or what strongly influences how you live your life?

Be your own biggest influence.

There is nothing wrong with taking your cue from other people whom you admire or even from the media. We are always changing and growing, discarding what doesn't work and trying to find what does. Heeding advice and tips from others is nothing more than your search for self-improvement. You can obtain usable information.

But the person who should have the only say in how you choose to live is you. Understanding that you are the only one who can allow or disallow anything that relates to your own life is an empowering feeling. No one in all the world can give this power to you; it is within you. Allow yourself to have the last word on what will impact your life.

QUESTION 5.
Can you reinvent yourself when your life is not going the way you planned or takes an unpleasant unexpected turn?

Reinvent yourself, be a risk-taker.

Reinvention is the real mother of change. Inside you are many different versions of yourself. No, you're not a victim of multiple personalities; nor are you entering the witness protection program! The various personas that make up "you" are normal and healthy.

Reinventing yourself is simply the ability to change when necessary. If one part of your life isn't working, say a job or relationship, it becomes necessary to make crucial adjustments. Is it risky? Yes, but the reality is that risks are a part of life whether we are crossing a street, driving a car, or making a change in our lives. We're always taking risks. But think about the alternative to taking risks. Our lives would stagnate. Risks allow us to grow. Think of taking a risk as opening a door to a new adventure. If the door closes, well, so what? You've had a learning experience if nothing else, and learning allows you to change and grow. Don't let a bad experience close you off from a life that can have happiness.

QUESTION 6.
Do you have happy memories of your past?

Make peace with the past.
While you cannot and should not live in the past, you will always have some memories of your life. Even in the worst time spans, there is bound to be one good memory. A horrible childhood has at least one precious moment when you were happy; a bitter relationship didn't start out that way. The problem is that we hold on to the terrible memories, and because they may be more numerous, they overshadow the few good ones we have stored on our memory chips. You need to bring the good memories forward and replace the bad ones that keep cropping up. Focus on one good memory from each part of your life whenever the bad ones surface.

A relationship with your past needs to be an acceptable one, a livable one. But your life should never revolve around past events, good or bad. Make peace with what was, plan for the future, but live in the present.

QUESTION 7.
If you are in an unhappy no-win relationship, are you willing and able to walk away no matter how difficult it may be?

End no-win relationships.

Nothing gets better by itself except perhaps the common cold—and even that takes a certain effort on your part. A no-win relationship that has no hope of ever changing is lost time in your life. And thinking that any relationship is better than none at all is a destructive way of thinking. What you are doing is permitting yourself to stay put just to be with someone who is not worthy of you.

It is amazing how we cling to a situation simply because it is all we know. It is seen in loveless marriages, abusive childhoods, and miserable work conditions. The idea that "things might change" is only wishful thinking. Do not lose time waiting for a change that will not come unless you take action.

QUESTION 8.
Finish this statement: "The way I am living right now makes me feel . . ."

Feel good about the way you're living or make changes.

If you answered "trapped" or "miserable," you need to stop, make a list of why you feel this way, and decide exactly how you can remedy the situation.

Animals feel trapped when they are kept from doing what is instinctive for them. Your gut instinct may be telling you that the time is coming when you will no longer be able to live this way. Don't hesitate in making a change as soon as is humanly possible. You are not alone. Don't be afraid to seek help in any way you can. There are free counseling areas in many local colleges that are specific to women's issues. Education, employment, job changes; help in all these areas and many more is available for women. Take advantage of what is out there to help you make changes.

QUESTION 9.
Where do you feel the most comfortable during the day?
Create a safe haven.
The place where you feel the most comfortable is your safe haven and your starting point for being happy. It should be a place where you feel distant from any unpleasantness or distress that the world has thrown your way. Use this place and time to view your life's situations as objectively as possible. From that vantage point you should be able to make decisions that will reap happy benefits for you.

A safe haven by its very definition is a place that is undisturbed. It is a place for you to daydream and make plans for those daydreams to come true.

QUESTION 10.
Do you allow your personal goals to always be postponed for other people?
Don't postpone your goals.
Rule number one—do not allow this to happen for any reason. Rule number two—repeat rule number one. Barring major illness or unforeseen and unexpected crises,

there is no rational reason to postpone your goals for anyone else all the time. You do not want to look back over a lifetime of should-haves and could-haves all due to giving in to another person's demands, whims, or fears.

QUESTION 11.
How do you really feel about yourself? Be honest.

Like yourself.

You can never get away from yourself. You can't take one step without bringing "you" with you! The many ways that people have tried to escape from themselves— through drugs, alcohol, or the like—have never worked. All that users have done is taken themselves on a danger- ous and fruitless trip. Using mind-numbing substances to avoid reality only adds to the problems already there. Ask yourself what exactly is it about you that you dislike. Don't play the martyr and say, "Everything." If there are specific parts of you that you don't like, decide if there is a way you can make some small positive changes. Big- ger changes can come later. Stop punishing yourself. You need to teach yourself to love and nourish you.

A healthy self-esteem and a reality check about who you really are is all you need. When that annoying little critic inside your head tells you that you're not worth that new car, a longed-for vacation, or an unexpected promo- tion, stop and ask yourself why you should feel this way.

The next time you feel that you are undeserving of something good, play another little mind game. Instead of listing why you're not worthy, turn the tables and ask yourself why you *are* worthy. Do not fall into the trap of negativity. Let go of past learned behavior. List three reasons why you are deserving and understand that by doing this you are teaching yourself how to take the first step toward a positive attitude.

QUESTION 12.
If you could magically go back ten years, what would you do differently?

Leave the past behind. Live in the present.

Get out the time machine! Of course you can't go backward in time to change something, but you can use that imagery to help you make your present better. Whatever you wanted to do ten years ago is more than likely still possible today in one way or another. There are no time limits save those you place on yourself. The fact is that whatever you wanted to do back then may be more possible now. You have maturity and, possibly, a better financial situation; you should be able to use both to your advantage.

We glorify the past and give it attributes it might never have had. See it for what it really was, warts and all, and leave it behind.

QUESTION 13.
At what age do you feel that it's too late for you to begin a dream?

Own your importance.

The right answer? The only answer? It is never too late to begin something that you have always wanted to do until you have "crossed over the bridge between life and death." In other words, when you no longer have breath in your body, then and only then is it too late. Don't see yourself as unimportant.

If we're asked to name the one person whom we feel is important in our lives, not many of us would say, "I am." Either we're afraid of being called vain, or we really do see ourselves as unimportant. Fortunately for us, the idea that we are not all that important is not true at all. That attitude is learned behavior and should be discarded immediately.

See yourself as the most important person in your life. You are not taking anything away from anyone else in your universe by believing this. You are not a bad person for believing it. It doesn't mean that you can't love anyone else or that you are narcissistic. It simply means that you value yourself as a person to be taken seriously and not treated as less than seriously by anyone.

QUESTION 14.
Finish this statement: "Before I can be happy, I need . . ."
Don't fear happiness.

Do you fear being happy? Maybe you've put it off for so long that it frightens you to think you've actually arrived at the moment of happiness.

You are unused to feeling anything but miserable.

Or perhaps you find happiness bittersweet. You are afraid to be happy because you've had moments of happiness in the past that were taken away from you or ended abruptly. You fear to allow yourself to be that vulnerable again. But there is more to the fear than simple vulnerability.

Fearing happiness because of a bad experience in life belongs in the I-don't-deserve-it category. We view joy being removed from our lives because we feel we didn't deserve it in the first place! We don't see the reality of a situation. A breakup, a major disappointment, an unexpected hardship—none of them are seen for what they really are, common life experiences. They are only seen as some type of punishment for not being deserving enough. It's a no-win situation. We'll never allow ourselves any happiness if we fear losing it.

QUESTION 15.
What is your definition of being wealthy?
Redefine wealthy.

Money may be a means to an end, but it doesn't guarantee happiness. All you have to do is read stories about lottery winners who believed that the fortune they won from a single ticket was their personal pass to happiness. It is not necessarily true. Despite the old joke that says, "People who think money can't buy you happiness don't know where to shop," monetary happiness is fleeting at best. There is no happiness guarantee where money is concerned.

While no one would say no to being financially well-off, true wealth is not what you have but how you use it. Using money as a means to help you achieve goals is one way to purchase a ticket for a better life. Money spent on your education is wonderful. Sponsoring your dream project is another way that having money can be used. Being wealthy itself is not the goal but a means to an end. Happiness and satisfaction are true wealth.

QUESTION 16.
What would you change about your life?
Let happiness become a habit.

There are going to be major changes and minor ones. Only you can decide what you need to do. Minor changes such as a small change in appearance or an exercise routine are relatively easy. Major ones, like changing the job you hate, leaving the relationship that is unhealthy, or moving to a different town or city, take time, effort, and planning. Life is constantly evolving. Inevitable changes such as aging will come whether you have made positive changes in life or not. If you're not happy, do not sit still and wait.

Happiness can become a habit. You just have to overcome the negative habits that stand in the way of making changes. Learn to weave a pattern of happy moments. You are the mover and shaker of your life; take positive actions.

QUESTION 17.
Do you think other people are happier than you? Why?
Focus on your own life.

It's a myth that others are happier than you. Sometimes the show of happiness is an act. Remember—you are living your life, not anyone else's. You have no idea what is really going on in another's daily life. Stop trying to find out their happiness secret.

When you put all your energy into trying to figure out what others have that makes them happier than you, it is the same as trying to watch a three-ring circus. You never fully focus on the center ring (your own life), because you're distracted by the activities in the other two rings. Stop worrying about why other people seem happier than you and focus on what is making you unhappy!

QUESTION 18.
If you *were* happy, how would you act differently?
Allow yourself to be happy.

Happy people *do* act differently than unhappy ones. For one thing, if you allowed yourself to be happy, you wouldn't constantly be kicking yourself for not being happy. People who are happy believe they are deserving. This makes them more generous to others in terms of kindness and compassionate actions; they make efforts to do more with their lives. If you are frustrated with your life, you become withdrawn and live as an outsider. You become a victim of your own negativity. You are worth much, much more than you realize. Allow yourself the power of feeling worthy.

QUESTION 19.
What is your emotional style when things don't go according to your plans?
Develop coping skills.

How you cope with situations has a direct link to your happiness. Understanding that some plans will go wrong, and knowing that there are always temporary setbacks when you do plan, enables you to create a valuable coping skill. Don't expect things to go wrong; that is a defeatist attitude. Expect the best but plan for mishaps just in case. Why do you think there are life vests on an airliner? The pilot and crew certainly aren't anticipating any problems, but they would be foolish to take off without making sure emergency equipment is in place on the off chance it's needed.

Slowly develop coping skills and a plan B that will allow some leeway if needed. Chances are good that you'll never need plan B—but it's good to know that you have it in place.

QUESTION 20.
What can you do to be happy right now and in the future?

Don't postpone happiness.

No one knows what the future holds for you. You can guess; you can consult an astrologer or psychic. But you need to assure yourself that you will be as happy *then* as you make yourself *now.*

By placing something in the future, you are unconsciously saying that you don't have to worry or think about it now. But you do. If you postpone being happy once it will become a negative habit which you will repeat over and over.

I am not going to be Ms. Sweetness and Sunshine and tell you that you should see everything through rose-colored glasses. That isn't practical. There are too many of us who go to jobs that drag us down or suffer interactions with very unpleasant people on a daily basis. There are pressing bills to be paid, family responsibilities to be taken care of, mundane, uninteresting chores to be done. Advising you to put on a happy face for everything is not reality. However . . .

Don't say you'll try to be happy. That way of thinking only means you aren't really serious about changes. And for heaven's sake don't assume that the future will automatically and miraculously bring you happiness. There is no magic wand that you will wave a few years from now and *boom!* suddenly all is right with your world. That's a surefire way of avoiding the present. You're postponing happiness because you don't want to think about it. If you think about it, then you have to act on it. Stop being like Scarlett O'Hara. Don't say, "I'll think about it tomorrow." Think about it today!

WRITE IT DOWN!

A good bit of advice about being happy is to:

Write It Down!

Sometimes writing down and charting a pattern can help you more than just thinking about it. On two separate pieces of paper, write down the headings HAPPINESS NOW and HAPPINESS GOALS.

Under HAPPINESS NOW write down what has made you smile, laugh, or feel good during your day. Record your daily happiness. This will show a pattern of good experiences, pleasant memories, and happy days. Then tackle your happiness goals. Write down what you want in the future. Think of this as something to strive for that in no way takes away your present capacity for happiness. In fact, goals can actually add to your present happiness if you see them as ways to improve your life.

If you'd like to change careers, write down how you'd like to achieve this and what you need to do to get to this goal. Be specific and realistic. Know exactly what preparations and additional education are needed. The HAPPINESS NOW paper will make you feel good every day and will become very important, because you will be creating a habit that will help you attain your future goals.

The paper for HAPPINESS GOALS should be read and edited as you work to achieve those goals. Like all actions and thoughts, good or bad, something becomes a habit only if we do it over and over again. You made a habit of your unhappy thought patterns; it will take time to create new habits to replace them. Be consistent in doing this.

Be the author of your own life and remember: All good writers edit. If something doesn't work, edit it until it suits you and you achieve your goal. Learn from yourself; you are both the teacher and the student.

THE FINAL KEY TO HAPPINESS: IDENTIFY REAL STRESS

There is one last key you need in your search for happiness: identifying and coping with real stress.

Everyone knows the definition of the word *stress*. And naturally, we think we know what is causing us stress. It is almost always from outside forces, of course. The plain truth though is that we inflict additional stress on ourselves without anyone's help. We make stressful situations infinitely worse.

Take a Break and a Breath

You can't catch your breath when you have to have everything "just right" before you can be happy. A colleague of mine used to go through her day breathlessly. She always sounded as if she had just run a race. Her pulse was fast, her heart would pound, she had migraines, and she could never catch her breath.

Concerned, she went to a doctor who could find nothing physically wrong with her, unless she counted the tight, contracted muscles my colleague had from self-imposed stress. Instead of giving her a magic cure-all pill, she sent my colleague to a yoga instructor.

After talking to the instructor, she found out that her problem was a simple one. Because her body was always so tightly wound up with stress, she had forgotten how to breathe correctly. Now, of course every living creature breathes; it is instinct, after all. But how you breathe, the technique of breathing, is as important as breathing itself.

The yoga instructor explained the problem very simply. Think about how you feel when you have a cold or allergy, he said. You can't get a good deep breath. This leaves you feeling lethargic and tired. Just getting through the day is a major challenge. Even a night's sleep isn't recuperative because you're not getting deep breaths. Not breathing correctly affects your entire body and your mind. That's why my colleague was breathless all the time.

He listened carefully as she told him about all the stress in her life, how every little part of her day added to the stress. After hearing her talk, he said something she wasn't prepared to hear. He told her there was one person in her life who was creating the most stress. She alone was that person. And he was right.

I am not discounting that you may live a life where there is an inordinate amount of stress. Many of us do. You can't help that because you are not responsible for stress caused by outside influences.

What you are responsible for is self-induced stress. Stress that you bring on yourself is more depleting than any other form. It is a "fake" stress, a learned and habitual reaction to uncomfortable situations.

Identify what your stressors are. In what way do you make the stress worse? Now ask yourself how you might be able to deal with them differently. Create one or two different scenarios for how you can deal with stress and try to use the best one. Not all stress is created equal; there are levels ranging from minor to major. Make a decision on how best to deal with the different levels.

The following are three examples of stressful situations that occur in many women's lives.

Pleasure stress has to do with something you want to do, are going to do, but requires a lot of details and some arrangements. Planning to go on a vacation produces stress even though we know that it usually will have a pleasant outcome. You can deal with this stress by envisioning the pleasure that lies ahead and knowing that good plans will provide the best vacation. Do all you can do ahead of time; avoid last-minute situations.

Workplace stress involves the D-word—deadlines. Deadlines at work produce stress because "it has to get done" no matter what. Deal with this stress by seeing yourself taking ten-minute hourly breaks and walking away from the project. If you say you *can't* do this, you are becoming your own worst enemy; you can, and you need, to do this. Ten minutes will not adversely impact the deadline. Ten minutes will help you keep fresh and more alert, enabling you to get it finished and over with.

Chronic stress is by and large family stress. This is the hardest to deal with because you are personally involved. It is difficult to avoid family members the way you might avoid unpleasant co-workers, but you can ease the stress by using a series of "don'ts."

Don't be the go-to person in every family situation, don't always be the peacemaker, and don't sacrifice personal time to deal with others' problems. You may not ever be voted best-loved family member of the year, but you will eliminate a lot of unnecessary personal stress by taking a stand on your own behalf.

Think about what your stress is doing to you physically. Some stress will always exist; there's no way to get around that constant in life, but the way you deal with it defines how you choose to live. It helps to remember that only a few stressful aspects of life have to be dealt with immediately or in a timely matter. Not all of them need your immediate attention.

When your health is adversely impacted and your ambitions are pushed to the side time and again, you are choosing a lifestyle that has nothing to do with gain and everything to do with losing. You're losing yourself to stress. When you put it into that perspective, it makes it much easier for you to . . .

Take a mental health day. These are "sick" days which are really just days off from work. You're not sick; you're just sick and tired and need a break from everything! You need to breathe deeply, take a step back, and evaluate what you are doing and how you can make a change that will be good for you.

Don't add stress to your life; there's already enough for you to handle. Take a break from stress and do something positive for yourself as often as possible.

NOURISH AND NURTURE: TWO SHORT STORIES

Make One Small Change, Make One Big Difference

Think about your everyday life. What is there that you can change for the better? What can you look forward to every day, even if it is something small? A woman named Claire made a change in her day just by stopping for a cup of coffee on her way to work every morning.

In a miserable teaching job with an administrator from hell, she had no desire to begin her day. Every morning she dragged herself to work feeling miserable. Stressed and angry all day long, Claire came home and did nothing more than vegetate on her couch. Her energy was sapped from all that misery. She felt trapped and discouraged.

Then one day she did something different but so simple. On the way to her dreaded job, she stopped at a gourmet coffee shop and bought a cup of coffee.

The clerk at the counter took her order, made it to her specifications, and gave her a freshly baked croissant as a free treat. The cup and the treat were put in a colorful little bag, and Claire was on her way to work with the fresh aromas of coffee and almond croissant filling her car. Alone in her classroom before the first bell, Claire sat and savored her treat.

Now, the trip to the coffee shop by itself did not change Claire's job; nor did it make the horrible administrator at the school any nicer. Those issues were, unfortunately, constants in her life at that period. But the impulsive stop was to have a kind of soothing effect on Claire in a different way.

Leaving her house fifteen minutes earlier just so she could stop at the coffee shop every day before school became a sort of sacred ritual. Claire was caring for herself, and this was key. The people at the shop were invariably nice, and Claire looked forward to going there in the mornings. She also looked forward to those fifteen precious minutes of alone time in her classroom where she sat and did nothing but drink her coffee and eat her croissant. By doing this Claire was nurturing herself and opening a window to a pleasant experience that would make her day a little easier.

Don't Blink—You'll Miss the Green Flash in Life

I have a very clear memory of missing out on a beautiful moment simply because I was too busy being preoccupied worrying about some now long-forgotten "mini crisis."

I was on the west coast of Florida with a group of friends who had all gathered to watch the spectacular sunsets famous in that area. In particular we were all waiting for a phenomenon called "the green flash," which can occur when weather conditions are just right. We were told that conditions that night were perfect. Though the phenomenon of the green flash is nothing more than a refraction of light in the atmosphere that creates a bright green glow on the water, it is an amazing, magical sight.

Scientific reasons notwithstanding, the green flash is rare and happens so fast as the sun dips under the horizon that if you blink, you will miss it.

Guess who blinked?

"That was incredible! Did you see that?!" exclaimed a man standing next to me.

I had to acknowledge that I hadn't. I, as usually happened in my life, was preoccupied and oblivious to the beauty around me. Though I went back to the beach for a week of sunsets, I never did catch a glimpse of the green flash. I saw it only in a photo someone took, which is nothing like witnessing the real thing.

Be attuned to your life as it is happening; you will never get back moments wasted on unimportant worries. Make the life journey happily memorable.

•••

Life happens fast; make sure you stop and catch the green flash.

The (Finally!) Attainable State of Happiness

Who are *you*?

You've read about women who have wasted major parts of their lives by feeling they couldn't be happy "until . . ." They sacrificed, put up with bad relationships, allowed others to dictate to them what was or wasn't successful, felt undeserving, and settled for less than they really wanted.

WHICH ONE ARE YOU MOST LIKE?

Debora and Sara, who waited for someone *else* to make them happy?

Belinda, who let jealousy *keep* her from being happy?

Elise, unhappy because she felt she wasn't successful enough?

Michelle, who willingly sacrificed her own pleasures and interests for her children?

Or Janet, who expected to live through her son's achievements?

Are you Estelle, who felt she had to be the perfect daughter and sister?

Or Anjali, who settled for everything and got nothing she really wanted?

Beth, the woman hoping that if she saved Daniel, they would both end up happy?

Or Lauren, who almost blew her life goal a second time by being both enabler and addict?

Do you relate to Caren, who postponed her happiness so often she almost missed finding it?

Are you Kimberly, who needed something more than motherhood to fulfill her?

Gillian, who was all work and no play and never said no?

Jenna, who was willing to live on the edge of her married lover's life?

Perhaps you are Cate, with a fear of trying and failing?

Or more like Alexa who didn't try at all?

Do you see yourself as Tina who was striving for impossible perfection?

Are you similar to Emma, who wasn't prepared for opportunity?

Or Heather, who didn't create an opportunity for herself?

Perhaps you're like me, the woman who deferred happiness because I felt I truly did not deserve it. Is that you, too?

All of us hoping for happiness sometime in the future when all of our "conditions" would somehow, miraculously, be met.

What happened to the women who were gracious enough and brave enough to share their stories with me? All had a vision of happiness that was derailed by their ideas of *what* happiness really was and *where* it was. I couldn't end the book without letting you know how they were doing.

During my original interviews, I asked each woman if I could contact her two years later for an update. Each one was willing to let me know how her life had changed. Each believed that in two years' time, that elusive state of happiness she was searching for would be hers.

Sara, Michelle, Anjali, and Caren corresponded with me by e-mail several times. They kept me up to date on how their lives were changing and what they were doing. It was good to be in touch with them.

I contacted the other women at the end of the two-year period, and all had endings to their original stories. How *did* all the stories end? Some ended on a positive note, and some didn't. Though life changes and two years pass quickly, it doesn't always have happy endings.

Debora and Sara were the women who were waiting for the men in their lives to change in order for they themselves to be happy. Debora did meet a man who was the polar opposite of Rob, and while she initially thought he was "too nice," she began a relationship with him that has shown promise. Because of her experience with Rob, she will always be careful of loving someone too deeply, but she told me that this man is good for her in ways that Rob never was. He appreciates her talents and her intelligence and gives as much as he gets in their relationship. So far, she says, they're a good match. Remembering what I said about there being some people with whom you would like to have a gourmet meal and some who don't even rate a cup of coffee, Debora says, "*This* guy is definitely worth a five-star dinner."

Sara was not so lucky. She's still married, still unhappy, but used to the "devil I know," as she puts it. That comment alone speaks volumes about how Sara unconsciously sees her husband. Though she frequently thinks about leaving him, she doesn't know if she ever will. When she understands that leaving a marriage is not giving up but giving herself a chance at a better life, then she will be ready. Until she *is* ready, her story has to be left at that.

The women who believed they were the have-nots have that same belief two years later. Belinda is still struggling with jealousy and finds that a happy life without a great deal of money is hard to come by. She feels she will never be satisfied with what she has and is still hoping that somehow more money will enable her to be happy. Where that money is coming from, she doesn't know. She only knows that money is her key to happiness.

Elise hasn't changed her dreams of international acclaim and sees herself as less than a real success. She hasn't been able to celebrate what she has accomplished because to her it is still not enough. These women may never change their ideas on what they need for happiness. They refuse to see that their ideas on the impossible and unattainable goals and conditions they set are actually ruining their chances for success and happiness.

What about our sacrificing mothers? Michelle did finally fulfill her dream and is happy in the small theater company where she is a respected member. She is learning to put herself first in her life. Her children, she says, are *not* happy with her decision and see her singing as a "hobby." Nothing is going to stop her, though; she is finally enjoying her life.

Janet, on the other hand, still feels lost and upset that she is no longer heavily involved in her son's life.

They have a relationship that is strained and not at all close. She doesn't understand why. Making a life separate from being a mom is very difficult for her because that is all she wanted and all she knows. There are times when she feels that there is some missing part of the puzzle; that she is to blame for the estrangement. The only answer she can come up with, however, is: "I guess I didn't do enough for him. I should have done more." Not having done enough is far from the real reason for the estrangement, but Janet won't accept that answer.

What about the "good little girls" Estelle and Anjali? Estelle has never left her parents' home, and chances are she won't anytime soon. Her mother became very ill six months ago, and her father needs Estelle's help now more than ever. There are days when she doesn't even leave the house and telecommutes to work. She still takes on all the obligations and asks nothing from her brother or sister. Estelle has become resigned to postponing her life indefinitely.

Anjali is living the independent life she wanted and making her own decisions in life.

"Right or wrong," she says, "at least they're my own choices."

She also told me she never settles for anything less than what she truly wants even if she has to wait to get it. Her new car is not something her parents feel she should be driving, but it is the one she *always* wanted and never got. She bought it soon after her divorce.

The women who were in toxic relationships are still rebuilding their lives. Beth who tried so hard to save Daniel went into therapy to help her sort out her conflicting emotions about leaving the relationship. She also discovered that she seemed to have an attraction to men with addictive personalities. This is something that she wants to learn to change.

Despite leaving Christopher, Lauren battled her own demons for more than a year when she found that she was unable to leave the alcohol behind. She had some difficult moments and dropped out of school again. Now in rehab, she is going back to school next year and determined to finish.

Caren is living her dream of studying in Italy. In an e-mail to me, she told me that no one should postpone a dream no matter what. Though she doesn't live with regrets, she does feel angry that she almost had to lose her life before she realized she was losing her dream. In postponing what she wanted to do, she was fair to everyone but herself. Caren's story touched me deeply. Her eagerness to tell her story, her wistful talk about the past, and finally her unabashed joy in describing living her dream was beautiful for me to hear. I am so glad she gave herself the chance to finally fulfill it.

Kimberly went back to her career. Her marriage went through some rough times, and she and her husband separated for a while. When they got back together, he grudgingly began to see that Kimberly was a happier, more fulfilled woman as a mother who works outside the home. Now he understands that a great mother can also be a person who is happy in her career.

She told me, "It *is* difficult balancing family and work, I have to admit that. But it is what I want and need to do for me."

Jenna almost became involved with another married man but stopped herself before she allowed it to go anywhere. She took a break from serious dating for a while and focused on just going out with nice, single guys she knows as friends.

But Jenna also admitted that she had slipped and had briefly rekindled the affair with Denis a year after he had left her. He had stopped in to see how she was doing—and that was all it took. Her feelings and physical need for him overwhelmed her and they were together for a few weeks until she broke it off.

The breakup came when he asked her if they were making a mistake by "beginning this again." Those words made her realize that it had to end, and Jenna knew that *she* had to be the one who made sure it was over for good. She told me that she couldn't live on the edge of someone else's life again. It was too painful.

Gillian, our workaholic, is happy in the small law firm and makes sure that she takes time to enjoy life outside work.

"It was a little hard downsizing my life to adjust to my lower paycheck, but it was worth it. Not having to say yes to a senior partner just so I could succeed in my profession has empowered me to have a personal life. I can't regret that. I feel better than I have in years."

Cate, who feared failure, is submitting her work. Even though she has received rejection letters from some art magazines, she has also gotten her photos into two small newspapers and an artists' catalog. She is not going to let her fear of trying prevent her from going after something that gives her a great deal of pleasure and fulfillment.

While the first rejection letter was hard to take and she was tempted to never put herself through that ordeal again, she didn't stop trying. When she received her first acceptance letter, she had it framed and keeps it on her desk as a motivator to keep trying.

Alexa still has days where she feels that she is doomed to fail; that attitude has worn a deep groove in her thinking and become a bad habit. But she says she's working on a more positive outlook ever since she had some small success at work. She is "trying hard to try."

Our perfectionist Tina, who had to collapse in order to see what an enormous burden it is to try to do it all and have it all, is learning to be just imperfect enough to slow down. For her, it like learning a new skill; she calls it learning to be "impossibly imperfect."

"I find it a bit unsettling, because trying to be perfect was the only way I knew *how* to be. It's easy for me to slip into that mind-set again. I *know* that I can't do it all well, but sometimes that's hard for me to *understand*. But I'm working on not letting that happen."

Emma has never forgotten how important it is to always be prepared for a wonderful opportunity. She makes certain that her skills are always impressive enough to be ready at a moment's notice to answer that knock on the door. It is paying off; Emma is in constant demand.

After several missed opportunities left her stuck in the job she so wanted to leave, Heather has finally put the pieces of her puzzle together. She created a new career as a personal travel and tour consultant, and it is working out well.

As for my own body image story, I make an effort every day to appreciate me for who I am and what I have achieved even if everything isn't "just right" and will never be. Happy was on hold for far too long.

Life has different tracks and paths, and every women must find the one that will take her to where she wants to be in her life. Each woman has to make decisions that will help her find her way to her own happiness. Are you making sure that you're on the right track to your happiness? You have to make a commitment; give yourself a push in the direction that will *allow* you to make yourself happy.

Will there be days of frustration? Certainly. Will everything go smoothly in your life? Certainly not. But during the journey, you need to know that you can have a definite say in how you travel. Doesn't it make sense to make sure you're doing what *you* want to do most of the time?

Absolutely.

In essence you really do become what you want to be if you can be positive in your thoughts. This is not meant to sound as if by "thinking happy thoughts" you can fly like the Darling children in *Peter Pan*. If that were the case, the world would be full of people flying high all the time! But reality proves that negative thoughts and attitudes are definitely not the ingredients you need to create happy moods.

. . . *And* Then *I'll Be Happy!* is meant to show you two very important facts. First is that, obviously, you're not alone in postponing happiness; the stories have shown you that it is a very common occurrence. And second: If you have learned anything at all from the stories and keys in this book, it should be that you have the right *plus* the ability to be happy. Those two combined are powerful components for a satisfying life.

You need to trust your instincts and feelings about real happiness and not a generic idea of when and how you should be happy. As with everything else in life, one size or one idea is not going to fit everyone.

Ask yourself: What makes me happy? Steve Jobs, the co-founder and CEO of Apple, Inc., told a reporter how he knew he was happy in his life. He always asks himself one simple question.

"If today were the last day of my life, would I want to do what I'm about to do today? If the answer is yes, that's all I need to know."

Don't disappoint yourself. One of America's favorite authors, Mark Twain, wrote a wonderful line concerning real disappointments.

"Twenty years from now you will be more disappointed by the things that you didn't do than by the ones you did do."

•••

From a former searcher for the elusive state we call happiness who thought everything—including the magic weight number—had to be "just right" in order for me to be happy, I can say that change *is* possible and happiness *does not* need perfection in order to exist.

And as is appropriate for a book about happiness and women, a woman has the final word. Asked who she felt was to blame for a woman's unhappiness, the great Katharine Hepburn answered,

We are taught you must blame your parents, your
sisters, your brothers, the school, the teachers—but
never blame yourself. It's never your fault. But, you
know, it's always your fault, because if you wanted
to change you're the only one who has got to make
the change happen for you.

Be the catalyst for your own explosion of happiness.
Make the change happen.

Be healthy, live fully, have goals, believe in you,
reinvent, prepare, rely on your own strength, create . . .
and *most* of all, be happy!

Index

H

happiness
  allowing, 203
  commitment to, 221
  dependence on others for,
    1–16
  as habit, 202
  insights, 191–212
  not fearing, 200–201
  ownership of, 12–14, 15
  permission for, 83–84, 93
  postponing, 204–5
  right to, 221–22
  taking responsibility
    for, 14
  waiting for, 31
  writing down goals for,
    205–6
Happiness Quiz, xxii–xxv,
  191–212
harassment, 148–49
have-nots, 17–31
having it all, 169, 172
healing and
  forgiveness, 102
health
  emotional, 44, 81,
    167, 176
  mental, 209–10
  physical, 167, 176
Hepburn, Katharine,
  222–23
hopes, 114
husbands, 1

I

identity
  reclaiming, 47–48,
    194–95
idleness, 175
imperfection, 167, 175
indispensability,
  142–47, 148
influences, 194
inner critic, 193
instincts, 222
investment, self, 81
irresponsibility, 68

J

jealousy. *See* envy
Jobs, Steve, 222
joy, 201

K

kindness, 104

L

laziness, comfortable, 184
learning, 195
limits, 169
living
  fully, 178–90
  in the moment, 119
  with purpose, 111
  within and without
    relationship, 14
love, 13
  of self, 14, 82, 198–99

and self-acceptance,
70–85
luck, 186

M
make-up sex, 105
managers, 120–21
marriage
   and affairs, 124–37
   arranged, 56–60
material possessions, 20,
   29, 201
memories, 105, 195
men, bad, 86–106
mental health day, 209–10
messiness, 177
Michelangelo, 85
Mildred Pierce, 32
mirror, 78–80
money, 17–22, 201
mood, 192
motherhood, 32–48, 118–19
   parent-child relationship,
      39–44
   and personal dreams,
      116, 122
   and personal life, 44–45
multitasking, 174

N
negativity, 81, 103, 150,
   159, 193, 199, 203, 221
negotiation, 121–22

O
opportunities, 178–90
other woman, the, 124–37

P
parenting, 32–48
parents, aging, 50–55, 65
past
   making peace with,
      195, 199
perception, 74
perfection, xi, 30, 167–77
   myth and reality, 172–75
personal life
   and motherhood, 44–45
   reclaiming, 150–51,
      194–95
   and work, 138–51
planning, 165, 186, 202
   and dreams, 107–23
pleasure stress, 208
positive thinking, 193, 199
possessions, material, 20,
   29, 201
potential, 163, 164
preparation, 186
priorities, 63
   dreams and plans,
      120–22
   and perfection, 175
   putting self first, 192–93
procrastination, 162
promises, broken, 87
purpose of vision,
   68–69, 111

celebrating, 24, 26, 29
combining with
motherhood, 47
and fear of failure, 165
increments of, 31
measuring, 25–27
personal, 17–31
and reality, 25

T
talents and gifts, 44
tenacity, 165
therapy, 101
thinness, 70–85
toxic relationships,
86–106, 196
trying, 152–66
Twain, Mark, 222

V
value, personal, 27
victim mentality, xi, 159,
161, 163, 203
vision, purpose of,
68–69, 111

vulnerability, 168, 200–201

W
waiting, 178, 185
wanting, 185
wealth, 201
weight, 70–85
well-being, physical, 84
Wilde, Oscar, 119
Winfrey, Oprah, 73
wishful thinking, 196
women
and affairs, 124–37
as caretakers, 49–69
dependence on others for
happiness, 1–16
trying to save bad men,
86–106
work
and personal life, 138–51
and stress, 208–9

Y
yoga, 207

About the Author

Kristen Houghton is a nationally syndicated columnist for Examiner.com, an affiliate of the Examiner Newsmagazine Organization, where her highly popular "Relationships" column reaches readers worldwide. She has been writing about relationship issues and how to live a personally successful life for more than ten years. Kristen is a frequent media contributor and speaker.

Believing that women and men can make personal changes that will enable them to live successfully and well, Kristen dispenses solid, practical advice to help her readers achieve their goals. Her innate ability to offer reality-based solutions to life's problems has garnered her praise from fans and critics alike.

She is a strong advocate for human rights, empowerment for women, and the National Literacy Program. Kristen also lends her support to the North Shore Animal League and Broadway Barks and is an enthusiastic patron of the arts.

As a well-respected educator, Kristen has taught International Languages and Cultures on the secondary school and university levels. Writing, however, has always been her first passion, and she was able to combine her love of words and language to launch a new career in journalism.

Please visit www.kristenhoughton.com for tips and stories on happiness and living successfully.

If you are interested in having Kristen Houghton speak to your group or organization on relationships or life issues, please contact her at: kch@kristenhoughton.com.